TALL TALES
AND
NO LIES

Coming of Age in the
Missouri Ozarks

John oliver wilson

Park Place Publications
Pacific Grove, California

Tall Tales and No Lies
Coming of Age in the Missouri Ozarks
john oliver wilson

Copyright ©2007 john oliver wilson

ISBN 978-1-877809-35-4

Printed in Canada
First Edition 2007
All rights reserved.

Published by Park Place Publications,
Pacific Grove, California
www.parkplacepublications.com

DEDICATION

*I dedicate my tall tales to my daughter, Beth Anne,
and my son, Benjamin Duncan. While not from the Ozarks,
they are of the Ozarks, where values run deep.*

CONTENTS

CONTENTS

INTRODUCTION

I GREW UP IN A PART OF THE COUNTRY where storytelling is developed into a fine art—the Ozarks of southern Missouri. It is not surprising that storytelling is a finely honed art in Missouri, given our tradition of producing great writers of tall tales, not the least being the best of them all, Mark Twain. So I grew up reading Mark Twain and listening to elders of my home town spin tales about their neighbors and their dogs, not always careful about distinguishing between the two.

When most people think of the Ozarks, they think of hillbillies and mules and country music. I never met a hillbilly. I knew a lot of people who might be characterized as having a Scots-Irish or German heritage with some French blood thrown in for seasoning. But we did-n't refer to ourselves as Scots-Irish or German or French, but simply as good down to earth folk. I certainly saw a goodly number of mules, most of them being of the two legged variety. Country music was not the highly commercialized tunes coming out of Nashville. It had roots deep in the more quiet and introspective side of Scottish and Irish folk music.

I have carried on the tradition of storytelling even though I long ago left the Ozarks. I have told the tales of growing up to my children and to close friends and to friends who were not so close. Indeed, to anyone who might listen. The tales have grown and expanded with the years, for true to my heritage it never bothered me to stretch the truth a little to engage listener interest.

This has not always gone unchallenged, for my daughter whom I am convinced is a female reincarnation of H.L. Mencken, has been known to so boldly state that, "Dad has his version of the story and the rest of us tell the truth."

I never found time to put my stories down on paper. And I guess I was a little gun-shy about drawing upon the experiences of my youth for story telling material for fear of being cast into that pile of literature known as "small town Americana of the best forgotten past."

The turf of small town America has been well plowed. Sherwood Anderson has written about his childhood at the turn of the last century. Thornton Wilder has forever embedded "our town" into our collective memory. Robert Ruark's *The Old Man and the Boy* is a classic story of values passed from one generation to the next. Laura Ingalls Wilder enriched the lives of countless millions of young and not so young readers.

These are not tales of a long forgotten past. They speak to me of concerns and values that each of us have simply because we are human beings: a desire for community, a recognition that education goes far beyond classroom walls, certain rites of passage that each of us must pass through on our journey from boyhood to manhood or girlhood to womanhood, and the people, mentors and institutions that give shape and values to our lives. It is these same concerns and values that I experienced in coming of age in the Missouri Ozarks.

I think the crusty old journalist had it right when he advised a young Ernest Hemingway in the art of writing: "As for subjects, the best are those drawn directly from personal experience."

As for rules of prudence in putting my personal experiences to paper, I must thank my wife, Beclee. When I first began the task of converting my stories from verbal to written form, Beclee laid down two rules.

"Rule number one," she informed me. "I will let you stretch the truth a little, for I know you far too well after all these years."

"And rule number two?" I queried.

"No lies!"

GATEWAY TO THE OZARKS

john oliver wilson

A TOWN CALLED ROLLA

I HAD THE FATE OF BEING BORN IN A small town called Rolla. I didn't choose Rolla, not that if I had the choice to make I wouldn't have picked Rolla. I might have picked St. Louis or Kansas City or even Chicago. Well known cities. Everyone has heard of St. Louis and Kansas City. "Meet Me in St. Louie" and "Everything is Up to Date in Kansas City." And who hasn't heard of Chicago. The city of broad shoulders according to no less an authority than Carl Sandburg. But who ever heard of Rolla. Not many.

You can't find Rolla in any Anthology of Great Place Names of the World. In fact, I don't think you can find Rolla anywhere else except on official Missouri State Highway maps. And then you have to search to find it. The name of Rolla is not printed in big letters that stare out at you like St. Louis or Kansas City or even Jefferson City (the capitol) or Springfield (down the road from Rolla). Even a small burg just nine miles to the east of Rolla carries the more stately name of St. James.

I always wondered why those first settlers in my home town had not done the same: St. Rolla. When I was growing up the local lore had it that the first settlers in Rolla hailed from elsewhere (not too surprising) and that they brought with the them names of the communities from which they had come (also not so surprising). One of those early pioneers was from Raleigh, North Carolina, and put forth the name of Raleigh. Whether those early settlers had difficulty in spelling or simply were speaking with the drawl characteristic of those from the South, no one really knows. No known record of what really occurred at the initial naming of Rolla has been found, if indeed one ever existed. However, the end result of the naming process was that Raleigh was recast as Rolla and no one ever bothered to set the record straight, for which I am eternally glad.

The local historians have a somewhat more embellished version of the naming of Rolla. John Webber, head of the first pioneer family to settle on the future site of Rolla, and two other pioneer families met to name the new community. Webber put forth the name "Hardscrabble," undoubtedly referring to his valiant attempts to eke out a living farming the local rocks. Another suggested "Phelps Center," reflecting the fact that the new community had just won the battle to be the county seat for Phelps County. This was clearly a pure political move. If the new county seat was named for the county then the possibility that the county seat might be stolen by St. James at some future date might be minimized. Fortunately, wiser heads prevailed for Phelps Center sounds more like a shopping center than a proud community. And apparently the wiser head was a man named Coppedge who suggested the name "Raleigh" provided that "it be spelled as he spoke it—R-O-L-L-A."

I never knew which version of the naming of Rolla was correct. Both seemed close enough that I never bothered to verify one or the other when I was being indoctrinated in Rolla history at the age of ten. It really doesn't matter much since the name of Rolla has survived for some 150 years and I doubt that it will be changed in the next hundred or so.

ROLLA: GATEWAY TO THE OZARKS

GEOGRAPHICALLY THE OZARKS ARE SAID by those who draw maps to stretch from the banks of the Missouri River on the north, to the Arkansas River on the south, to the Mississippi River on the east, and almost to the Kansas border on the west. It is a vast territory of some thousands of square miles that are inhabited by a sprinkling of small towns—no cities of any worth.

However, the exact geographical bounds of the Ozarks are probably best left alone for as one local once wrote on the subject, "the question of the boundaries of the Ozarks should be debated in the spring when the blood has thinned and the hide thickened."

If the geographers are right Rolla has no legitimate claim to being the "Gateway to the Ozarks." That honor would probably belong to Jefferson City. So the residents of the state capitol by all rights should erect a sign high on their banks overlooking the Missouri River that "Jefferson City: Gateway to the Ozarks" lies just ahead.

Fortunately, the locals of my home town were not about to let the state capitol claim the title as "Gateway to the West." That honor by all rights belonged to Rolla, even though Rolla lies some 60 to 70 miles as the crow flies to the south of the purported northern border of the Ozarks. Rolla had one big advantage over the state capitol. That advantage was Route 66.

Old Route 66 did not meander its way along the banks of the Missouri River on its way west from Chicago and thus give Jefferson

City legitimacy as the "Gateway to the Ozarks." But rather it plunged straight down through the cornfields of Illinois headed to East St. Louis. There it crossed the Mississippi River and began its long journey southwest across Missouri towards the Oklahoma border. About halfway across Missouri it cut a path right through the north edge of Rolla. This did not go unnoticed by the local entrepreneurs of the time. They quickly erected large signs just to the east of town announcing to those headed west that "Rolla: Gateway to the Ozarks" lay just ahead.

It was down old Route 66 that Dad and Mother motored one bright spring day in late April of 1936 as a newly wed couple. They had spent their honeymoon in St. Louis shopping for linen and dishware and cutlery and all the other essentials for setting up housekeeping. Passing the gateway sign, they turned south on Pine Street and made their way to a newly rented apartment a few blocks from the center of town.

Sporting a newly minted degree in Agriculture from the University of Missouri, Dad had been employed by the U.S. Department of Agriculture to serve as regional head of Production Credit in south-central Missouri. This meant that he had to travel throughout the Ozarks appraising farmers and their crops to assess their qualifications for government loans.

In 1936 the Depression was still in full swing. Farmers in the Ozarks had always struggled with the land to eke out a living and the Depression did not help. As the saying goes in Rolla, it was hardscrabble farming at best. For those not from Rolla, hardscrabble farming means that rocks stand a better chance of growing than does corn or soybeans. The Depression just gave the rocks a better chance. And with so many rocks the farmers didn't have to worry about drought and wind storms lifting the soil from the earth and depositing it elsewhere as was true in the plains of Oklahoma. Rocks are hard to budge, even by the worst of dust storms.

Dad represented the federal government, never a very popular institution in the Ozarks. After all, the Ozarks were a great source of bootleg liquor and the federal "revanoouers" were viewed as something akin to weasels or skunks. But that was some years past. FDR and the New Deal were known even in Rolla and the federal government was gradually coming to be seen in a new light. The U.S. Department of Agriculture along with the U.S. Department of Forestry and the U.S. Bureau of Mines were seen as major institutions doing good. Dad was stationed in Rolla to do good.

Doing good did not necessarily mean appraising potential crop yields, carefully assessing the local farmers projections of crop output and expected crop prices, examining books and questioning production and fertilization plans. Appraising in the Ozarks meant walking the fields, getting to know the farmers and their kinfolk, where they came from and what they valued. It meant drinking coffee around the pot-bellied stove in the kitchen, scratching fleas from the head of the birddog sprawled on the floor, and commenting on the quality of the homemade apple pie. Contracts and loans were executed with a shake of the hand. And Dad shook a lot of hands in those days.

Mother was of a different cut than Dad. She also hailed from northwest Missouri. But whereas Dad was born and raised in Maysville, a small farming town in DeKalb County, Mother was a city girl. She had grown up in St. Joseph, or St. Joe as Missourians are prone to say. St. Joe was a little rundown by the time I arrived, but in times past it was a proud center of finance and commerce. It had a rich past. The Pony Express originated from St. Joe with the first leg of the journey west to Sacramento starting from a big wooden barn still standing near Katy Park. Jesse James hailed from St. Joe. Jesse and his brother, Frank, cut a large swath through the imagination of young impressionable Missouri boys, myself included. Whether outlaw or Robin Hood did not matter. Numerous wagon trains also set out from St. Joe. And so there was a lot of history that would at a later date stir my imagination when we made the trip back to visit Aunt Blanch and Aunt Dorcus and a host of second cousins.

Mother received her education at the University of Missouri as well, majoring in journalism. She was very proud of the fact that she was a journalist from Mizzou. The university has a well deserved reputation for turning out first-rate journalists. Mother was also a debater in college. And she was blessed with a razor sharp mind. So the combination of investigative reporting and debater tenacity along with a mind that questioned everything and everyone was not well suited for life in a small Ozark town. There were no large newspapers like the *Kansas City Star* in Rolla. There was no Prendergast machine in Rolla that offered a young investigative reporter fodder. But Rolla became her home for the bulk of her adult life. And so she decided to focus her drive and energy on a large family. That is where I came into the picture.

WE'LL KEEP A GOOD EYE ON HIM!

A T THE TIME OF MY EARLIEST RECOLLECTION we were living in a small white frame house on West 10th Street, obviously from the street name on the west side of town. The house sat back from a dirt road that ran due west past the Anderson's and the Wilkins' and the Jackson's and into the woods. Not many houses stood between us and the Ozark hills. My first recollections of life were oak trees and woods. Bobby, two years my senior, and Jackie, three years my senior, quickly introduced me to my new environment. I was shown a secret path through the woods and across a creek and then alongside a bank where we constructed a lean-to out of stripped oak saplings that Bobby and Jackie cut down. This became our place of retreat and hiding and dreaming and playing Indians.

At the bottom of West 10th Street, just a short walk from our house, lay Route 66. I had yet to learn that Route 66 was legendary, made famous by the likes of Dorothea Lange who photographed and Woody Guthrie who wrote songs and John Steinbeck who penned novels about those who traveled up and down the highway. All I knew was that West Elementary School lay on the other side of Route 66 from my house, and I had to cross the highway to get to first grade.

I didn't make this trek on my own. Nan, Jackie's older sister, picked me up on her way to sixth grade. Hand in hand, we worked our way down West 10th Street, heading for West Elementary School when I wanted to head into the woods for the lean-to. However, building character in Rolla did not include cutting school at the age of six. I must admit that I sort of looked forward to Nan's arrival and our departure for school for a lot happened on our way that was more interesting than hiding in the lean-to.

World War II was then in full swing and down Route 66 from Rolla lay Fort Leonard Wood. It was the main training base for the U.S. Army Corp of Engineers as well as basic training for young Army recruits. With luck, Nan and I would arrive at the bottom of 10th Street just in time to be trapped by a long convoy of Army trucks and armored vehicles and large guns being towed behind even larger trucks and sometimes great big giant tanks. For a six year old this was great stuff. The trucks were full of soldiers yelling and cheering to our waves as they passed. They threw out bubble gum, a rare and highly valued commodity in those days. Often, by the time the convoy passed, we were late for school. Almost in time for first recess.

My circumscribed world of woods and lean-to, Nan and Jackie and Bobby and Route 66 was soon greatly expanded. I was about to be introduced to the broader community.

"Pete, time for your first real haircut," Dad abruptly announced early one Saturday morning on a warm September day. No more getting my hair trimmed by Mother. I was to get the real thing. And so I was taken, hand in hand by Dad this time, walked down 10th Street past the intersection with Route 66 and on into town. We were heading for the Modern Barber Shop on Pine Street.

Pine Street was the main street of Rolla. It ran from the north end of town where it connected with Route 66 to the south end of town where it petered out at the Frisco Railroad tracks. It split the town in half, one half lying on the east side of Pine Street and the other half lying on the west side of Pine Street. Rolla had no uptown or downtown or high rent district or wrong side of the tracks. You either lived on the east side of town and went to East Elementary School, or lived on the west side of town and went to West Elementary School.

Along this route through the center of town lay nearly all of the businesses of importance to the life of Rolla and to my early life as well. It was here that the leaders of the broader community held court. And a major center of court was the Modern Barber Shop. The barbershop fronted Pine Street with big picture windows that gave a clear view of the comings and goings up and down the main street. No local, tourist, young boy or stray dog could venture through Rolla without coming into clear surveillance by someone in the barbershop. It was a gathering place of those who simply wanted to chew the fat and argue local politics with no intention of getting their hair trimmed.

The barbershop was owned by J. Nean White, who also owned Modern Cleaners right next door. An internal doorway connected the two so one could drop off cleaning and immediately repair to the barbershop without having to go outside. But more importantly it served as a passage for Mr. White, as I was soon to learn, to address one of the more influential members of the community, a way to keep an eye on both of his commercial enterprises. Nean White, as Dad referred to him, was one of Dad's closest friends. This I did not know while being led hand-in-hand for my first encounter with the broader community and my first real haircut.

"Well, J.R., you're bringin' that son of yours in for his first real man's haircut," Mr. Geers greeted us as we entered the barbershop. Mr. Geers held forth on chair number one—the chair closest to the surveillance picture window and the one that denoted rank and seniority among the three barber chairs arrayed along one side of the shop with wooden chairs and a long bench alongside the other.

I sat on the wooden bench next to Dad in quiet anticipation of what was in store for me as Mr. Geers brushed off the cuttings from his chair from his previous customer. He then reached back of the counter and pulled out a wooden board, which he laid across the arms of the barber chair.

"O.K., son. Hop aboard and let's get started," Mr. Geers directed me with a big smile and a helpful hand to mount the chair. I took my place perched on top of the board and waited in more anticipation. With that Mr. Geers took a large white bib of an affair, snapped it in the air, swirled it across my chest and secured it around my neck. Next came the electric razor up the back of my neck. I nearly jumped off my perch with the first feel of a vibrating electric razor going up my neck.

"Hang in there, son. It don't bite," admonished Mr. Geers. "You need to sit solid and still or I might miss and take off an ear or two. Now that wouldn't look too good to your mother. Don't you think?"

The thought of losing an ear to two gave me pause. I braced up my back and sucked in my breath for my next encounter with the vibrating electric razor going up my neck. I soon adjusted to my first exposure to a real man's haircut and wondered what I was going to look like once Mr. Geers had done his job and received Dad's approval. Before final inspection time, Mr. White came through the door from his cleaners and greeted Dad.

"Well, J.R., what do we have here perched on the chair. That young one of yours?'

"Yep," replied Dad.

"Well, he looks like he might turn out to be a good one," Mr. White proclaimed after carefully looking me over as I sat imprisoned with the big white bib tight around my neck and the fear of losing an ear or two keeping me frozen in rigid position on the board.

"Yep," replied Dad again.

"Well, it's good to meet John, Jr. We'll keep a good eye on him for you, J.R."

With that, Mr. White retreated into his cleaning shop and it began to dawn on me that there were other forces to contend with in the broader community of Rolla other than my immediate family, Nan, Bobby, Jackie and the lean-to.

FIRST METHODIST CHURCH

I GREW UP A METHODIST. DAD WAS a Methodist. My grandfather was a Methodist. My great-grandfather was a Methodist. So it was naturally assumed that I would be enfolded into the Methodist Church as well. I didn't mind. It seemed to me that the Methodists of Rolla were the leading citizens. Not that the Methodists had a total monopoly on leading citizens, for the Presbyterians were also in the running. But their little white clapboard church on the east side of town, far removed from the center of town, didn't seem able to compete with the large red brick structure of the First Methodist Church. Our church was planted on 9th and Main Street, a couple of blocks west of the center of town and a few blocks south of the School of Mines campus. It was well located for keeping a careful eye on business and academic affairs. Leaders from both communities were represented in the church membership.

Methodists arrived in Rolla in 1862, convinced Edmund Bishop, the founder of Rolla, to donate land for a new church building, and opened their doors. At the same time a Rolla Sunday School was established under the charge of the Methodists. The Sunday school was open to members of all denominations. It had "a good library of books and it was better for the boys and girls of town to attend it than to run loose on the wild and dirty streets."

Rolla, being situated in a border state, had more than its fair share of Southern Baptists. And the Southern Baptists could stir up local politics something awful when they took such a notion. They were certainly a force to contend with.

Catholics were also present in fairly large numbers. They built a massive church, by Rolla standards at least, out along Route 66 at the north edge of town. And they provided the only kindergarten in Rolla in my day. So I can claim some Catholicism in my background since I attended their kindergarten for one year. When the Catholic kids were hauled off for Mass, or whatever they did in the church, we Protestant kids were left behind to fend for ourselves. So I never got indoctrinated into Catholic beliefs. Not that it would have worked, for the First Methodist Church was not about to lose one whose lineage ran so deep.

Sunday School at the First Methodist Church was command performance. It was a given that I would spend the better part of each Sunday morning being indoctrinated into accepted Protestant Christian beliefs. I assumed that this was the normal way of life. I was many years away from any serious questioning of standard Christian doctrine. However, those questioning seeds were well planted on my first encounter with Sunday school.

I must have been around eight at the time. My mother dressed me in what she felt was the appropriate garb for attending Sunday school. One simply didn't go to Sunday School at the First Methodist Church costumed in the blue jeans and flannel shirt that were my official uniform at West Elementary School. I was dressed in wool gray shorts, a newly pressed and overly starched white shirt that cut into my neck, and a dark blue blazer.

I was not too pleased with the thought of being garbed in this new uniform, for it brought back memories of an earlier encounter in my young life when dressed in similar clothes. And that had not been a pleasant experience, to say the least. That encounter occurred on my first day of kindergarten.

Mother, being from the big city of St. Joe, assumed that the appropriate dress for a young boy attending kindergarten was knickers and high socks, and little black leather shoes. I arrived at kindergarten and stares and snickers greeted me immediately upon my entrance into the classroom. It didn't take me but one quick glance around the room to notice that I was the only boy in such a uniform. Not having a change of clothes in the lunch pail that I was clutching in my hand, I had no choice but to sit down, carefully keeping my eyes focused straight ahead in an attempt to ignore my surrounding classmates, hoping for the best.

The "best" occurred in the first recess break. It was delivered in the form of a great big bully of a third grade kid named Sammie. "Hey, little sissy, what's-a-that your a wear'n? I think we need to dress it up a little with some dirt." With that introduction, he summarily proceeded to knock me to the ground, shove my face into the dirt and give my clothes a good roughing up. Needless to say, the next day I appeared in the accepted uniform of the day: blue jeans and flannel shirt.

So, no wonder I had a certain feeling of fear and trepidation when I walked up the stairway to the second floor to my Sunday school room. However, being eight and more worldly wise in the ways of playground survival, I was prepared to defend myself a little more aggressively this time. But, with one quick glance, I observed that I was not the only boy so garbed. I was in good company. I took my seat at the table with ten or so of my fellow Sunday school mates. With a big sigh of relief, I began to take in my new surroundings.

Along the walls of the room were pictures showing various scenes of Jesus. They were held up with big thumbtacks in the four corners. The pictures must have been there a long time for they were curling up at the edges. It was obvious I was not the first kid to encounter those Biblical scenes.

Directly in front of me was a large picture of Jesus sitting in a field of green grass and yellow daisies surrounded by little children and some sheep. Jesus was lily white with light brown hair hanging down to his shoulders and clear blue eyes. I was struck by his face, which seemed very angelic, calm and serene. He was holding out his hands towards the children who were also lily white with light brown or blond hair.

I thought this a little strange since Mother had told me that Jesus had lived far away in a place called Jerusalem, in the Middle East, and that the people of Jerusalem were dark skinned and dark haired. I had pictured Jesus as a rather tough looking fellow who was challenging the oppressive rulers of Rome. I assumed that I would be able to resolve these conflicting views once Miss Miller, our Sunday school teacher, arrived.

Miss Miller came in with an armload of papers and leaflets which she immediately passed around to each of us. These were our Sunday school lesson guidelines and material for the fall. We were instructed that we would begin with a reading of some verses from the Bible. We would then have a little discussion of what these verses meant to each of us. And then we would turn to the lessons to see how those who prepared the material interpreted the verses we had just read. With that introduction, Miss Miller opened her Bible and began to read.

"In the beginning God created the heaven and the earth. And the earth was without form and void; and darkness was upon the face of the deep. . .and the evening and the morning were the first day. . .and God made the firmament. . .and the evening and the morning were the second day. . .and God said let there be light. . .and God made the beasts of the earth. . .and God created man in his own image. . .and God saw every thing that he made was good. . .and the evening and the morning were the sixth day. Thus the heavens and the earth were finished."

"Any questions?" asked Miss Miller.

I immediately shot up my hand, wanting to know what those Bible verses had to do with the picture of Jesus with the small children. But Billy beat me to the punch.

"Yes, Billy, what did you learn from the Bible verses?" asked Miss Miller.

"Well, Miss Miller. That is not what my dad told me."

"And what did your dad tell you, Billy? Please share it with your classmates."

"Well, my dad told me that the earth was formed from gases and stuff that was swirling around way out in the sky. That stuff gradually came together to form the earth and other planets like Mars. The earth was hot and liquid and then it cooled and hardened. It was all covered with water. Then land began to come up from the sea and form the hills that we see around us in Rolla today. He said all of this took billions of years, not six days. So why did the Bible blow it?"

We bolted to attention. I looked at Billy with a new sense of respect. This was really getting good. Sunday School was not so bad after all. Boy, was I going to have some questions for Mother when I got home!

Miss Miller sucked in her breath and turned to Billy.

"Now, Billy, your dad has told you one of the ideas about how the earth was formed. And we just read another. Each of us is free to choose which one we believe. I am sure that as you get older you will decide for yourself which one is right. But I happen to believe that the one in the Bible is right."

I later learned that Billy's dad taught geology at the School of Mines. Even later I learned that geologists took a different view of the creation of the earth than that related in the Bible. But at the time I thought Miss Miller gave a good answer. It was the same answer I got at home later from Mother. But to this day I think Billy's dad was one smart fellow!

ST. PAT COMES TO TOWN

St. PAT IS THE PATRON SAINT OF IRELAND. He is also the patron saint of Rolla. That may seem a little stretching of the truth. Ireland and Rolla! What do they have in common? I once found a four-leaf clover in our backyard, but that hardly counts for St. Pat status. And the closest thing to an Irish pub was way down in St. Louis, a hundred miles east on Route 66. But to anyone who grew up in Rolla of my day, it was obvious. St. Pat had somehow found his way from the green hills of Ireland to the oak hills of the Ozarks. How this miraculous event occurred takes some explaining.

Somewhere along the line to sainthood, Patrick the missionary became patron saint to engineers. To this day I don't know how this connection occurred, whether St. Pat embraced engineers or maybe engineers just embraced St. Pat. No matter. What does matter is that by the time I came along St. Pat was fully ensconced as patron saint of the Missouri School of Mines and thus of Rolla.

Each year, as the long, cold icy winter of the Ozarks was drawing to a close, St. Pat's Day would beckon as the rite of passage into spring. It was a time when the miners, as the students at the Missouri School of Mines are known, would cut loose and for one long week celebrate the exuberance of youthful life. Those of us still too young to be miners did not let a few years of maturity keep us from embracing the same feeling of exuberance. We anticipated St. Pat's Day second only to Halloween.

Apparently, St. Patrick walked around the hills of Ireland on his pilgrimages carrying a crook. A crook is a rather thin rod of wood with a hoop on top that I assumed in my youth was used to grab wayward Christian souls by the nape of the neck and pull them back into the fold. I am sure theologians attach a more refined concept to the crook.

But the thought of young freshman miners who bore the brunt of their first initiation into the rites of St. Pat's Day running around campus carrying a slender crook did not do much for the image of tough mining engineers. So the slender crook was converted to a sizeable felled oak tree of some forty to fifty pounds with the large knob of the rootball serving as the hook. The St. Pat initiates, and all freshman students were by definition initiates, were required to carry their shillelagh as it was called around with them at all times. Pity the poor initiate who happened across some upperclassman without his shillelagh over his shoulder.

St. Patrick was also blessed with an escort, or spirit, or a soulmate by the name of "Victor," according to Irish bards. Now Victor accompanied St. Patrick everywhere, and so our St. Pat had to have his own escort as well.

On the anointed day of St. Pat's arrival by hand powered railcar, that is, March 17th, several hundred shillelagh armed initiates along with a thousand or more upper classmen, Rolla citizens and the entire population of younger male youth of Rolla would gather at the old Frisco train station to await the arrival of St. Pat. His exact time of arrival was a carefully guarded secret shared only by his trusted escort "Victor." But the rumor would spread that it would occur at a given time plus or minus an hour or so, thus ensuring maximum buildup of anticipation.

The elders of the town would stand and peer down the tracks. We younger ones would put our ears to the rails to listen for the transmitted sound of iron wheels rolling over iron rails, having read that Indians and train robbers had mastered this technique. Soon we could hear the sound of the hand pumps and the grunts of the pumpers who pushed up and down in unison to the commands of the crew chief. . . "heave down mates". . . "now pull up mates". . . "put some meat on those poles and keep this thing movin'."

St. Pat would be standing with wide spread legs in the center of the platform surrounded by his anointed bodyguard. Our St. Pat was no heavenly angelic creature. He sported a full beard, was tall and broad of shoulder, clutched a large, thick staff of oak, and looked tough and commanding. He arrived and promptly stepped down onto the platform with the command: "Let the parade begin."

With that command, the Missouri Miner band would strike up an Irish march, the military color guard would unfurl the American flag, the Missouri State flag, and St. Pat's personal flag, which was white with a large green shamrock embossed in the middle, surrounded with smaller shamrocks around the edges. On up towards Pine Street and the center of town we all marched, heading for campus. There waiting were the floats that had been carefully designed by the various fraternities and clubs of the campus, all intricate in their design with moving green hats, shamrocks, snakes, leprechauns, and all kinds of engineering paraphernalia. Being hands-on engineers, these floats were marvels of movement and design.

The parade snaked down Pine Street, circled back towards fraternity row and up towards campus. At the conclusion the shillelagh armed initiates gathered at 8th and Pine, the center of town, heaved their shillelaghs into a big pile, and St. Pat ignited the whole pile to the roar of the surrounding crowd.

The miners then adjourned to their fraternity houses and clubs to begin the serious celebration of drinking green beer, dancing with the local girls and carousing into the wee hours of the night. While off limits to younger ones, this did not prevent us from trying to sneak in for a continuation of the celebration. But there was always a strong armed guard at the doors to the fraternities and the clubs to keep the local youth at bay.

On Saturday night the big ball took place at the old Jackling Gym. St. Pat and his attendants arrived with the St. Pat Queen and her court. The girls were all dressed in long low cut gowns and full skirts. Local residents attended dressed to the hilt. A dance band was imported from St. Louis. This was the height of the social season for the elders of Rolla, and the culmination of months of anticipation for the younger set of Rolla.

I don't know if Victor is still around after these many years, but I would like to think that he is. And I am sure that he would greatly approve of St. Pat extending his missionary efforts to the Ozarks, and in particular to Rolla.

GASCONADE RIVER: AND THE
GREAT GREEN MONSTER

THE GREAT GREEN MONSTER IS NOT THE Gasconade River, although it could easily refer to the river. Not that the Gasconade is a monster. It does run green at times, along with dark blue, sometimes black, and even yellow after a heavy rain has washed some Missouri topsoil into the stream. In this case the great green monster is a canoe, my canoe in fact. I built it when I was halfway between fourteen and fifteen. Home designed and home built, it was a beauty of a canoe if I dare say so myself.

I didn't name it the great green monster. That came later once it was built. But it was rather big as far as canoes go. Most canoes are sleek little vessels, 15 or so feet long, narrow at the girth, light on the shoulder, fast and mobile in the current. Only the voyageurs of the far north woods and lakes built great big hulking cargo canoes for hauling their tons of beaver and other furs across the great lakes, so I had read in "Boy's Life." Most canoes are those nice shiny aluminum Grumman things that I learned to paddle my way around in at Boy Scout camp.

I even had earned the Canoeing Merit Badge at Boy Scout camp. So I knew how to get in and out of a canoe, how to paddle it forwards and backwards and sideways, and how to launch it from a pier. But the pier at Boy Scout camp was on the side of a great big swimming pool. And there was not much room for paddling around in the swimming pool. My canoe was destined for much bigger water—the Gasconade River.

The Gasconade River, according to no less authorities than Lewis and Clark, is a "river that falls into the Missouri from the south, one hundred miles from the Mississippi. Its length is about one hundred and fifty miles in a course generally northeast through a hilly country. On its banks are a number of saltpeter caves, and it is believed some mines of lead in the vicinity."

Wow! Lewis and Clark seemed to have learned an awful lot about the Gasconade River having spent just one night encamped "on a willow island" in the middle of the muddy Missouri River at the exact spot where the Gasconade River enters. And they weren't there to do any exploring up and down the Gasconade.

I suspected when I first read the Lewis and Clark journals that they got all their information from some Osage Indian warrior, for there were a large number of such warriors running around the territory at the time. The journals make note of "between twelve and thirteen hundred" Osage warriors in the area. Undoubtedly, some of those warriors had actually traversed the Gasconade, maybe as far downstream as the area around Rolla. I could hardly wait to see what those warriors had reported back to Lewis and Clark.

But first I had to get the green monster built. And that took some doing. I did my homework on the fine art of building a canoe, Indian style. This wasn't going to be one of those fine East Coast pleasure canoes of Old Town fame, the ones with beautifully constructed ribs and fancy woven cane seats. Indians, so I had read, paddled their canoes with their butts propped against a hard crossbar, knelling on the bottom of the canoe. From this position they could easily maneuver the canoe through raging rapids or in close for combat or for whatever. And so my canoe was going to be built Indian style: no seats. Just strong crossbars and a wooden bottom deck for knelling purposes. This proved to be no problem in my early design. However, some of the other aspects of building an Indian canoe did pose some problems, serious problems.

Indian canoe makers start out getting the material for their canoe, which was birch bark. They would find some great big birch tree just waiting to be peeled of its outer skin, generally in the spring when the bark is soft and supple. The birch bark comes off the tree in massive size, sometimes pieces twenty feet long and four feet wide.

Unfortunately, the Ozark hills don't sport very many large birch bark trees where bark can be readily peeled off in the spring twenty feet by four feet. In fact, the Ozark hills don't have any birch bark trees that I ever came across in my wanderings. And oak bark makes a poor substitute for birch bark as I soon learned once I tried to peel a great big white oak tree down near Beaver Creek south of Rolla. So I was stumped. Without birch bark and no good substitute, how was I going to build my Indian canoe?

Fortunately, *Popular Mechanics* came to the rescue. My latest issue arrived just in time. In it was a feature article on how to build your own canoe using marine plywood, copper screws, heavy duck canvas, and many coats of dark green marine paint. Now these were materials readily available in the Ozarks. Marine plywood was no big deal. Powell Lumber Company carried this as a matter of course for the many johnboats that any bass fisherman worth his salt could readily construct in his garage. Copper screws were part and parcel to the flatboat construction. Heavy duck canvas could be ordered by Hazel Dent up at Dent's Dry Goods store on Pine Street. Dark green marine paint was available in any number of locations.

My major problem, upon carefully reading the *Popular Mechanics* instructions, was how to get the canvas skin tight and keep it skin tight on my canoe once the keel had been laid, the ribs put in place, the slender side slats softened and copper screwed around the frame, and the marine plywood attached to the bottom. The solution lay just to the north of Rolla where the old airport was located.

The airport had seen better days. Now the hanger held a few private Piper Cubs, a machine shop for tuning engines and installing new propellers, and a gas pump for fueling purposes. But at one time it had been a major place of early flight activity. While that activity was now little more than a few flights by locals on weekends, of far greater importance to me was an old barrel of gook sitting at the back of the hanger. I guess the gook was used to coat the canvas skin of some of those old planes. At any rate, the gook was still pliable and useable. A few empty gallon paint cans purchased from Powel Lumber Company, a half dozen trips out on my bike and back to our garage, where I was carefully stockpiling the necessary materials for my canoe, and I was in business.

My canoe building was a carefully guarded secret. I shared my dream only with Mickey, my buddy who lived across the street. I needed some help in getting the keel laid true and straight on the sawhorses I had carefully made for holding the frame of the canoe.

I would also need some help in getting the canoe out the door of our back family room—the old farm kitchen now converted into a play space for our growing family. I figured "play space" included building a canoe, so I did not give much thought to how my folks might react once they got wind of my project. Mickey and I plotted the day when we would haul all of my materials out of hiding behind the shed, lay out the keel and attach the main ribs to the keel on top of the sawhorses, and begin the process of installing the side slats.

The day arrived one warm spring evening when my folks were going to the annual Rotary Club dinner. Dad was then President of the Rolla Rotary Club, and I figured I could count on him being absent on this critical day. Once they were out the door, I beat it across the street to summon Mickey to get started. We worked furiously all evening. By nine that night we had the main body of the canoe all laid out on top of the sawhorses. Mickey went back home and I climbed into bed, full of excitement and visions of paddling my way down the Gasconade in a matter of a few weeks. I was just about to doze off when I heard a soft knock on my bedroom door.

"Pete, you asleep in there?" Dad asked.

"Not yet, Dad."

"Well, then, how about coming downstairs with me and tell me what's going on in the back room?"

Oops! I bolted out of bed, drew on my jeans and beat a hasty path down the steps and into the back room. I saw Dad on his knees, eyeing down my keel to see if it was laid out true and straight. He rose from his knees and carefully walked around the frame on top of the saw horses, testing each rib to see if it was securely fastened to the keel. Then he ran his hands over the siding to see if it was true. All of this seemed to take an endless amount of time.

I stood quietly in the doorway, watching Dad do his thing.

He turned to me and said: "Well, Pete, quite a project you got underway here."

I saw a slight twinkle in his eyes. A grin began to creep across his face. So I knew I wasn't in too deep a trouble.

"How do you intend to get this thing out the door once you get it done?"

"Dad, don't worry. I got that carefully figured out. While it may look big sitting there on the sawhorses, I can squeeze it sideways through the back door."

Mickey and I worked hard over the next few weeks. The ribs and side slats were quickly secured. The bottom decking of marine plywood was screwed into place. The heavy duck canvas was stretched taut over the frame, given a couple of coats of gook to draw it even tighter, and then painted with four coats of dark green marine paint. Launch day was fast approaching. All we had to do was get the canoe through the back door.

Mickey and I carefully removed the finished canoe from its perch on top of the saw horses and carried the canoe sideways towards the back door. Something had gone wrong with our measurements. Try as hard as we could we could not squeeze the canoe through the doorway. That was no big problem, we thought. Simply remove the door jams. A couple of crowbars and hammers later we had the door removed and were fast at work taking out the door jams themselves. That is when Dad suddenly appeared on the scene.

"You boys figure to take out the side of the house as well?"

"Well, Dad, we got a little problem here," I answered.

"I do believe you do. Got any solutions in mind?"

"Not yet. Do you?"

"Well, I always did think we needed to put a large picture window in this back room. Let in a little more light. Bet if the two of you were a little more careful with your tape measure you might be able to build me a new picture window and get that big green monster of yours out of here at the same time."

It was clear that Mickey and I didn't have much choice. Launch day on the Gasconade was put off for a couple of weeks until we had sawed our way through a maze of lathing and plaster, carefully cutting a large opening for the picture window and getting it installed and sealed up. That was a small price to pay for getting the canoe and me to where we belonged—on the river!

EDUCATION IS
SERIOUS BUSINESS

john oliver wilson

MOTHER: DEBATER FROM MIZZOU

I AM THE PRODUCT OF THE ROLLA PUBLIC School system. Point of fact: East Elementary School (class of 1950). Rolla Junior High School (class of 1952). Rolla High School (class of 1956). Honor student and Salutatorian of the class of 1956. Point of clarification: I slipped up and got an A- in second semester Biology, sophomore year. Mary Kay did not slip up. She was Valedictorian for the class of 1956. I have made a point of not speaking to Mary Kay at every class reunion since.

We took education pretty seriously in Rolla when I was growing up. The local school board elections generated more heated debate and voter turnout than any other elections of the times, with the possible exception of the U.S. presidential elections. And then it was a close call as to which election was more important. Teachers were highly regarded and were reasonably well paid, given the times. School bond issues were relatively easy to pass. A new modern high school was built in time for my sophomore year and we had our own fully equipped chemistry and physics laboratories. Since there were only six of us in my class taking chemistry and physics, it was what you might call "one-on-one" education. We were expected to study and to perform. No room to slack off. Hard to avoid at a six-to-one ratio.

However, this is not the real story of my early education. Good as the school system was, dedicated as the teachers were, and supportive as the local community may have been, my early education really began on the home front. It began being shaped by my mother.

"Son," she called from her upstairs bedroom. "Would you mind making me some tea and toast and coming up to the bedroom. I have something I want to discuss with you."

Mother never called me by my nicknames of Buster or Pete. Nor did she use my given name of John. I was always "Son." She called me Son from the first days of my remembrance until the day she died.

I was twelve years old at the time. Mother was spending most of her time in the upstairs bedroom recovering from pneumonia. She had been hit pretty hard by the disease.

It had only been a few weeks since that my sister, Pat, and I were called into her bedroom to say good-by. Dad and the family doctor were standing by her bedside. The doctor took us aside and whispered to the two of us that he did not think Mother was going to live.

We knew she was seriously ill, but had no idea that we might lose her. The shock was so great that we just stood there, the two of us holding hands as tightly as we could to keep from shaking. Then we were led one at a time to her bedside. When my turn came Mother turned her head towards me and drew me nearer with her hand.

"Son, take good care of your father for me and look after your sisters. Promise."

So when Mother asked me to bring her tea and toast and come up for a discussion, I was jumping inside with joy. She had survived. She was still with us. My world was once again whole. I quickly delivered the tea and toast and climbed up in bed beside her.

"Son, as you well know, the war is long over," she began. "But a lot is happening in Europe and around the world. You need to understand this."

She went on to explain to me what Communism was all about and how Stalin had negotiated agreements at Yalta that were reshaping the world in the post-war era and how the United States was going to be tested in the future. It was my first lesson in geo-politics. It was but the first of many lessons that I was to be given by Mother over the next couple of years.

Mother's idea of lessons was not nice quiet discussions sitting in bed with tea and toast. No. Lessons were debates—hard hitting, well researched and reasoned arguments, no holds barred. Mother had been a debater all through her high school years at Central High in St. Joseph and all through her college years at the University of Missouri. Debate was in her blood and she loved nothing more than engaging in a good confrontational debate, no matter what the topic, or where the setting. It must have made for some interesting social encounters when she first arrived in Rolla.

I guess she missed her debater days at Mizzou and I was to become the substitute for the colleagues that had challenged her mind back in college. So debater I became. And in the process I found my educational learning curve moving to a higher intensity than in Rolla Junior High.

"Son," she announced one morning after breakfast had been cleared away, "I need to explain to you debating. A topic is selected nationally each year and all high school debate teams engage on this same topic. You have to be able to represent both sides of the issue, arguing the pros and cons on whatever issue is selected for that year."

I wondered to myself where all of this talk about debate was headed, since high school was a couple of years down the road and I was fully occupied just trying to get through junior high school. But I knew it was futile to bring this up for once Mother set her mind on a course of action, nothing would deter her. So I was given orders to construct a speaking podium. I was sent to the workshed for that task, and being somewhat handy with tools I was able to construct a reasonably passable speaker's stand. This was immediately placed in the middle of the kitchen and Mother took her position seated in a chair directly in front of me about ten feet back.

"Now this is where the judges will be sitting," I was told. "They will be listening to not only your arguments, but they will be watching your posture and your gestures. What we call stage or speaking presence. So you have to learn how to stand and speak directly to your audience. You won't have a speech to read from, although you may have some notes on the stand with you. But no one wins debates by burying their head in notes. So you must learn to think on your feet. Now we have to select a topic for you to begin researching." And with that I has given a topic and sent on my way to the Rolla Public Library to begin the task of researching and developing my arguments.

It was pretty rough going in those early days. I stuttered and slurred and fidgeted and coughed my way through the early sessions at the kitchen speaker's stand. Mother was patient, coaching and encouraging me in my stage presence. But she never let me lose sight of the fact that debates are won and lost on substance more than on form. And so she would look at the pro and con arguments that I had been carefully researching and preparing and rip them apart. Back to the library for more research and deeper thought. Again to the podium in the kitchen. More instructions and guidance and back to the library. The months passed and I was given new topics to research, refining and honing both my research and speaking skills until I was ready to join the Rolla High School debate team.

Mother did well by her son. I began to collect trophies throughout southern Missouri. My bedroom bookcase was fast filling up with proof of Mother's success, along with my head. I was beginning to think I was pretty hot stuff, maybe even hot enough to become a debater at Mizzou. That was until I ran into a kid named Billy down in Joplin, Missouri.

Billy introduced himself to me before we engaged in the regional finals of the American Legion Speaking tournament to debate the topic of "Should the United States Do Away with the Electoral College System." Unfortunately, he forgot to mention that he was also an ordained Southern Baptist minister who could call upon the Almighty, whether the pulpit be in a church or at the regional finals. He took me to the cleaners. I limped back to Rolla High School with my head several sizes smaller than when I had left for Joplin. Sorry, Mizzou.

GREAT AUNT LOU: LEARNING MY SHAKESPEARE

HER LEGAL NAME WAS LOU P. MCADAM, which is by husband number two. By husband number one she was known as Lou E. Putnam. Mr. Putnam, as she always referred to husband number one, was the local banker in Maysville, the small town (even by Rolla standards) in northwest Missouri where the Wilsons hailed from. Great Aunt Lou married husband number one very early in her life, buried him while still quite young, and moved on with her life. Great Aunt Lou was never one to dwell much in the past. Life going forward was much too exciting to be bogged down in the past. And good it was that she took this practical, down-to-earth approach to life, for she lived to be 96.

According to her obituary, Great Aunt Lou was born in the old Lytle Hotel in Maysville on January 2, 1870. She was one of four girls born into the Wilson family, the one and only boy being my grandfather. This made her aunt to my father and great aunt to me.

I was the tender age of ten when I made my first trip to Maysville for what was to become a traditional Memorial Day gathering of the Wilson kin. Now one just didn't go up to Great Aunt Lou and call her "Auntie." One had to be briefed and coached for the upcoming meeting of the youngest male member of the Wilson clan with one of the most revered and highly regarded elders of the clan. So, before my first encounter with Great Aunt Lou I knew that she had started teaching school at the age of sixteen. By the time she was in her early twenties she had earned both a bachelor's degree and a master's degree in English at the State Teachers College in Greeley, Colorado. And she had taught in Central High School in St. Joseph (some years prior to my mother attending Central High), taught school in Kansas City, and then returned home to Maysville where she became principal of Maysville High School. She was eventually elected Superintendent of Schools for all of DeKalb County, rounding out a career of 50 years devoted to teaching. Clearly, she was a force to be reckoned with.

I must confess the first sight of her left me standing in somewhat speechless awe. She stood mighty tall, at least from my short perspective at that time. Her figure was quite full, not fat, but firm and commanding. She had a large head capped with pure white hair. Her blue eyes snapped and sparked as I felt her gaze sizing up this newest addition to the family. She stuck out her right hand, grasping mine very firmly, and pronounced: "Welcome, John Oliver. I am delighted to finally meet you."

From that day forward I was never referred to by Great Aunt Lou as other than John Oliver. And she pronounced John Oliver in such a way that I always felt, being the youngest and only male member of the younger set of the Wilson clan, that I was expected to do the family proud. And doing the family proud was learning my Shakespeare.

Great Aunt Lou was a Shakespeare scholar. To her way of thinking William Shakespeare was the greatest mind to ever be unleashed on the world at large. She majored in Shakespeare at the State Teachers College in Greeley. She taught Shakespeare at Central High in St. Joseph and Maysville High in Maysville. At the age of 80, long after she had retired from active teaching and administration, she enrolled in a graduate class in Shakespearean Literature at the University of Kansas at Lawrence. Rumor had it among us kids, us kids being my sisters and cousins, that her home on Main Street in Maysville contained one of the largest collections of books on Shakespeare in all of Northwest Missouri.

It took me a couple of annual Memorial Day pilgrimages to Maysville before I was ever invited into her library. The library was located just to the right of the front entrance to her large Victorian house. She always kept it locked and off limits to all guest and visitors and new family members. It was her private space for reading and thinking. I guess Great Aunt Lou finally decided I was worth keeping in the family, and I was given an invitation to visit with her in the library.

"John Oliver, after we clear the table of the breakfast dishes and you wash up, I would like to see you in my library," Great Aunt Lou quietly announced early one Spring morning on our annual Memorial Day pilgrimage.

I carefully knocked on the door to the library and waited until she announced: "Come on in John Oliver."

I slowly opened the door, not knowing what to expect, and quietly closed it behind me. Looking around I found myself in a moderately sized, octagonal shaped room completely lined with bookcases. In the middle of the room sat a large wooden rocking chair. Off in a far corner was a writing desk covered with papers and books and pictures of past classes, and other assorted accouterments from her teaching days. I stood just inside the doorway trying to take all of this in and wondering what was to happen next.

"Sit down," Great Aunt Lou ordered, motioning with her hand

that she wanted me to take a seat on the floor in front of her rocker. She was in the rocker holding a book. Once on the floor I was handed the book: *Macbeth*.

"Now start reading."

"Where?" I queried.

"Act I Scene I, of course. It begins like this. . .When shall we three meet again? In thunder, lightning, or in rain? When the hurly-burly's done, when the battle's lost and won. That will be ere the set of sun. Where the place? Upon the hearth. There to meet with Macbeth."

She rolled these words off her tongue as if she were standing on the stage of a great theater. The words were full and deep and resounding. The hair on the back of my neck stood straight up. She not only knew *Macbeth* by heart, she knew *Macbeth* deep down in her soul.

"We're going to learn *Macbeth* together," Great Aunt Lou said rather matter-of-factly.

"You must start by reading *Macbeth* out loud to yourself, listening to the words as they flow through your mind and out your mouth. Shakespeare is verbal. All good writing and storytelling is verbal. First you must get the words. Then you can begin to put those words down on paper."

MUSIC: THE TRUMPET MAN
FROM SACRAMENTO

His name was George L. Walrath. I always called him Mr. Walrath. But when he first appeared on the scene in Rolla he was simply known as the trumpet man from Sacramento. At least that is what the powers to be of Rolla called him when they gathered at Long's Coffee Shop on Pine street for their midmorning coffee break. Dad was a member of the powers to be.

Rumor had it that George L. Walrath came to Rolla from Sacramento in California. It was sometime in late 1946 or early 1947 when he arrived. No one was sure exactly when. But without any notification of the powers to be, or any advance warning, Mr. Walrath opened a coffee shop on Route 66 where West 10th Street crossed the highway. He named his coffee shop the "Cal-Mo Café," obviously playing off the name of the state rumor had it he came from and the name of his newly adopted state.

Mr. Walrath was also rumored to be a great trumpet player from California, hence the handlebar given by the powers to be. He was said to have played with Herbert Clark and to have studied under the great Mexican trumpet player Rafael Mendez. And it was duly noted that he had let it be known, when approached by one Rolla power, that he no longer was in the music business and definitely was not interested in giving trumpet lessons to any Rolla youngsters.

This was a blow to Rolla, for music was very important in town life. Rolla had its town band, its School of Mines marching band, and its Rolla High School marching band. But the music program in the Rolla public schools needed improving, at least in the minds of the locals. So a new and more aggressive bandleader was hired, with the mandate to develop a good music program throughout the entire public school system. It was to begin in grade one and continue through grade twelve. And above all else, he was to produce a high school marching band of which Rolla could be proud.

Mr. Kite, the new band director, immediately opened a summer music program in anticipation of the fall, and began recruiting. I was among those recruited. I had just turned nine. On a long table Mr. Kite had arranged a number of shiny brass instruments: cornet, trumpet, French horn and trombone. A tuba was perched on a metal stand on the floor beside the table. I hit upon the trumpet as my instrument. But being young and still physically small, Mr. Kite suggested to my parents that I start with the cornet, which is smaller and easier to hold. And so I left clutching a well-used cornet in a black vinyl case as a loaner from the high school music department.

That fall and into the early spring I went for music lessons several days a week from East Elementary School across the back playground to Rolla High School. Between classes, I sat up in my bedroom at home practicing scales and small bit pieces. Progress was slow and tortuous, or at least that is how my folks and our nearby neighbors put it.

The consensus was that I needed lessons, and the sooner the better! So one evening over dinner, right after the arrival of Mr. Walrath, Mother turned to Dad and posed the question:

"Do you think Mr. Walrath might be prevailed upon to give our budding cornet player lessons?"

"I don't know. But it is certainly worth a try before our neighbors rise in revolt and we lose our minds," Dad responded.

I didn't much care for his answer, but I was in no position to argue otherwise. Furthermore, I wanted to take lessons with the hope of improving faster. I held my tongue and sat tight awaiting the next move.

Several days later I found myself packed into the car with my loaner cornet beside me. Mother drove me across town to where Mr. Walrath lived. It was a small square box of a house, sitting in a development surrounded by other small boxes of houses. We walked up the front sidewalk, rang the doorbell, and were ushered into the living room by Mr. Walrath. The room seemed dark coming in from the bright sunlight and I squinted my eyes trying to adjust and see what was in store for me. All I could focus on was a very shiny and beautiful trumpet hanging from a cord tied to the light fixture in the middle of the room. The trumpet was hanging down to about my height. I thought this very strange indeed, but said nothing.

I stood still, waiting. Mr. Walrath had his hands clasped behind his back as he looked me up and down. Then he slowly walked around me without saying a word and came back to my front.

"I think he'll do," he said to Mother. Then he turned to me.

"Son, I understand you want to take trumpet lessons."

"Yes, Sir," I answered.

"And I understand you have been playing for some time," he continued.

"Only a few months," I hastened to answer not wanting him to think I was better than I really was. I leaned over to open my cornet case thinking he wanted to see how well I could play or not play.

"Don't bother with your horn," Mr. Walrath instructed. "I want you to play a note for me from the trumpet hanging from the cord."

I glanced at him rather puzzled by this command, but I walked up to the trumpet and started to grab it with my hands to hold it tight against my lips.

"No hands," Mr. Walrath said.

What do you mean no hands, I thought to myself.

He continued. "I just want you to walk up to the trumpet without holding it and blow me a note."

I did as I was instructed. I walked up to the trumpet, took a big deep breath, blew out my cheeks full of air, placed my lips against the trumpet, and let loose. The trumpet sounded a great big air filled blurt, swung away from my face and swung back into my face hitting my lips hard. I backed off, rubbing my hand over my hurting lips and waited for the next encounter.

Mr. Walrath said nothing. He slowly raised the cord holding the trumpet to his height, stepped back and then moved into position. One hand was still clasped behind his back and the other hand gently holding the trumpet to his lips. He blew the most beautiful note I had ever heard. It was clear and full and firm. No quivering. No shimmering. No sound of air hissing from his lips. Just a pure, beautiful note that resounded off the living room walls and into my ears.

"Now that is what a trumpet should sound like," he said to me quietly. "Do you want to learn how to play notes like that?"

"Yes, sir."

And so my lessons with Mr. Walrath began. He laid down some rules. I was to practice a minimum of one hour a day. I was to practice standing up, holding my horn straight out in front of me. I was to plant my feet solidly beneath me, center my body in my groin, take a deep breath filling up my diaphragm and then slowly and firmly blow the air up through my throat and into the mouthpiece of the horn. I was to think of the air as going in a straight firm line through the horn and out the front bell towards some distant point—a wall or a tree or some other object off in the distance. I was to think of the air as flowing from the depths of my diaphragm through my body and horn, as if they were one aimed at some distant object. No blasting. No filling my cheeks with air like a chipmunk. No forcing of air or tone. Just pure sound. Quiet and clear and round and full.

I was Mr. Walrath's only student. We started with weekly lessons, and then as I made faster progress we would meet twice a week. I rapidly improved as our neighbors were quick to note. I advanced my way through "Abran's Complete Conservatory Method for Trumpet," beginning with the first studies of whole notes, progressing through scales in andante, and then a little faster scales in allegretto, and then even faster scales in allegro. I learned the slur and the double tongue and the triple tongue. I mastered some of the great trumpet fantasias and airs and "Trumpeters Lullaby" and the "Hungarian Melodies" of Vincent Bach.

It was early spring of 1949. Mr. Walrath and I had been at the trumpet business for nearly two years. I now owned my own shiny new Conn trumpet. One lesson day Mr. Walrath told me that a talent scout from the "Ted Mack Show" in Chicago would be coming later to hear me play. He explained that the "Ted Mack Show" was a great opportunity for young musicians to become known.

Scholarships to schools of music might be forthcoming. We

talked about a career in music for the first time. But when he saw the concerned look on my face he quickly reassured me that such decisions were far in the future. He and I still had many years of learning and practicing together before I had to think of careers and possibly music school. I was much relieved.

The talent scout arrived. I played Hungarian Melodies and several other pieces which he recorded. He then explained that the recordings would be sent back to Chicago for review, but that we should expect to hear from the Ted Mack Show. I was what he called a "child prodigy" on the trumpet. I had never been called that before. My chest filled up with pride at the thought.

Once the talent scout left, Mr. Walrath gently brought me back to earth.

"Now, son, we both know you are good, but we are going to take it slow. You have a lot to learn and a long way to go. Forget that child prodigy stuff. Enjoy your music while you are still young. Music is to be enjoyed, when you are young, when you are middle-aged, like me, when you are old. You should enjoy music your entire life, whether you make it a career or not. If the "Ted Mack Show" pans out, you and I will ride the train together to Chicago. It will be a great experience. If it doesn't work out, it doesn't matter. Now let's get back to work."

I was in the fifth grade at East Elementary School that year. It was towards the end of the day and I was sitting in my seat waiting for the final hour of school to begin. It was April and we had just come in from recess. I noticed Mother at the door to the classroom motioning to our teacher. She stepped out into the hallway to speak to Mother and then came back into the classroom to my desk. She gently put her arm around my shoulders and leaned down and whispered that my mother wanted to see me outside.

Mother took me by the hand and led me out of the school build-ing. Then she turned to me, holding both of my hands in hers, face to face.

"Son," she said. "I have some difficult news for you." She paused. "Mr. Walrath is dead."

I just stood there stunned, trying to absorb what I had just been told. I didn't know what to say, and so just blurted out: "Mr. Walrath . . . dead?"

"Yes, he died of a heart attack this afternoon at the café," Mother said.

She put me in the car for the short three block drive home, not saying a word. I stared out the car window trying to hide the tears streaming down my face. Mr. Walrath was like a grandfather to me and we had so much going for us. I couldn't believe he was gone. I thought about all of our lessons together, his softly encouraging talks when I was feeling down, his warm smile and arm around my shoulders each time I arrived for a lesson. I felt a great big pit forming in the bottom of my stomach.

The next day Mother received a telephone call from the Walrath family wanting to know if I would play taps at Mr. Walrath's service. Mother said she would check with me and get back, but she was sure that I would want to play. I was not sure what this involved, but a member of the American Legion Post in Rolla came over to explain to me how a military service was conducted.

It was a cool day in early April after the church service when we took Mr. Walrath to Rolla Cemetery. His gravesite was on the down-side of a hill in the middle part of the cemetery, looking out over a field and off into the rolling hills of the Ozarks. The wind was chilly, even though the sun shone bright and clear in the blue sky. The casket was covered with an American flag. The family was seated on one side of the casket in chairs. The military honor guard stood on the other side of the casket standing at attention. Three or four members of the military honor guard stood off to the side holding rifles at attention. Upon command, they raised their rifles to shooting position and fired three volleys to honor their deceased comrade. The honor guards firing the rifles were members of the Army ROTC unit at the School of Mines. After the final volley was fired, it was time for me to play taps.

I stood holding my trumpet in front of me as the graveside service progressed, trying to keep warm. I was more than a little scared with the thought of my part in the service about to come. I ran through the notes of taps in my mind, wanting to make sure that my mind wouldn't suddenly draw a blank when I put the trumpet to my lips. I wondered if I would be able to sound the notes loud and clear, or would they come out muffled.

The last volley sounded. I put the trumpet to my lips. Suddenly, without warning my legs started to shake and my hands began to quiver and I felt panic swell up in my head. Then I remembered Mr. Walrath's message from our first meeting. Plant your feet firmly. Center in your abdomen. Breathe deep into your diaphragm and let the air flow slowly and firmly up through your throat and into the mouthpiece and out through the trumpet. And aim for a far distant spot.

I planted my feet firmly in the ground, rose to my full height and breathed as deeply as I could. I looked over the heads of those at the graveside and focused my mind on the far distant hills of the Ozarks.

Then I blew. The notes came from down deep. They were clear and full and firm. Beautiful notes. The last notes I would ever play for Mr. Walrath. And I knew Mr. Walrath was pleased.

VALUES: LEARNING THE GAME OF GOLF

Dad was a golfer, as were just about every other adult male in Rolla. It was not that Rolla sported a country club, or a golf course with well manicured greens, or a golf pro or any of the trapping to be found on the big courses in St. Louis or Kansas City. Nor was it that the Rolla males played golf as a means of broadening contacts, doing business, or being seen with the "right people." The Rolla males played golf as a lesson in life itself. This lesson I was soon to learn.

The golf course in Rolla is situated at the very western edge of town where the School of Mines some years ago had carved out fairways among the oaks, put in sand greens, and converted an old equipment shed into a "clubhouse" for the use of the students and faculty. For an annual fee of $125 the locals were allowed to join the club. And for local kids the annual fee was cut to $25. The School of Mines knew that a good many of us local kids would eventually find our way to becoming Miners, and they wanted to let us know we were welcome, even on their golf course.

As soon as the weather turned warm in early April, and the ground had hardened up from the long winter of ice and snow, Dad and the others would head to the golf course on a Sunday afternoon after church to do justice to the game of golf. In my early years, I was left at home as too young to learn the game of golf. But it wasn't long before Dad announced one bright spring morning on the way home from church:

"Pete, want to come along today and tote the bag?"

"He's too young to be carrying that great big heavy golf bag of yours," Mother immediately interjected.

My heart sank. But Dad saved the day.

"Now, Honey Dear, don't get your dander up. He won't hurt himself. So, do you want to come along?"

"You bet," I hastily answered before Mother could say anything else.

Nothing more was said as we drove home. After a quick lunch I ran to the garage to get Dad's golf bag. I hosted it on my shoulder, but the bag was nearly bigger than me, heavy with clubs and totally unbalanced. All the clubs fell out as the bag turned upside down. I was busy on my hands and knees trying to stuff the clubs back into the bag, trying to figure out which particular slot they went into, when Dad suddenly came through the door.

"Let me give you a hand there, Pete. I'll be carrying the bag. I never intended for you to do so. I just thought you might want to start joining me and walking along with the rest of the men. Do you some good to get out."

We threw his clubs into the back-end of the pickup, drove up West 10th Street past our old house, and pulled into the parking lot. Mr. White was already there, talking to a couple of other men I knew. This was Dad's foursome. They had played together for some years and didn't seem in any mood to stop now.

"Well, you got that young one of yours with you I see," Mr. White addressed Dad.

"Yep."

"Good to have him aboard. About time he started to learn the game," Mr. White concluded. With that he came over, stuck out his right hand which I had already been taught to grasp firmly in return.

"Welcome."

"Thank you, sir."

And with that the four men grabbed their bags, threw them up on their shoulders and marched off for the first tee. I quickly ran to catch up and tried to match their step, one for one.

I spent the summer "totin' the bag," as Dad called it, when invited on a Sunday afternoon to join the foursome. I never assumed that I was a full-time, permanent member of the foursome. That would have been much too presumptuous at my age at the time. It was by invitation only. But the invitations came with increasing regularity and I would have been crushed not to have been included. I suspect that Mr. White and the others would have been disappointed as well for they seemed to embrace my company as a matter of fact.

The next summer proceeded along about like the first summer. "Pete, you want to come along and tote the bag. . .Yes Sir!. . .Good to see you again this summer. . .How did the school year go?" And off we would march to the first tee. By now I was a head taller than the year before, infinitely older, and far more mature and developed. It was time for me to quit "totin' the bag" and begin to grasp one of those clubs in the bag and see what I could do, at least to my way of thinking. It must have been to Mr. White's way of thinking as well, for one hot Sunday afternoon in mid-July he suddenly said to Dad.

"J.R. Don't you think it's about time we got John, Jr. his own set of clubs and set about teaching him how to play?"

I could hardly contain my surging joy. Yeah, you're right Mr.

White…enough of this totin' stuff…I need to get my hands on those clubs and get started…time's growing short. . . I thought to myself. But I had to wait for the verdict from Dad.

"Yep. I think you're right. Better pick him out a club or two when we finish the round," Dad responded.

I was ready to conclude the round on the spot. Call it a draw. Call it even, or whatever, settle up the score and flip to see who was going to buy the cokes at the clubhouse. No need to suffer through another nine holes plus adding up all the scores to determine the losers, and the coke buyers, when something as important as getting my first set of golf clubs was in store. But the game had to be concluded according to rules and tradition.

The rules and the tradition were rather complex. No playing for par. No match playing. Too boring. Rather the Rolla males played by a set of rules known as "prox, putts, low ball and low total." Two men to a team. Two teams to a foursome. One point went to the team whose player drove closest to the hole. A second point went to the team with the lowest total putts. A third point went to the team whose member had the lowest total score. And a fourth point went to the team with the lowest total score for both players. If a team swept all four points, their team would be awarded a bonus point. So it was possible to win five points on each hole. That meant that there was a possible total of 90 points to be divvied up in an 18-hole game.

At the end of the game the foursome carefully examined the card of the official scorekeeper of the day to make sure that everything was in order. Since the task of being the official scorekeeper had fallen to me by then, I was always careful to make sure that the points for prox, putts, lowball and low total were accurately recorded after each round.

Not that I had to worry for fear of being wrong, for each player well knew where he stood in the scoring as the game progressed. But they seemed to keep their own private score cards well tucked away in their brain cells, only to be disclosed if the "official score card" did not mesh with their own "private score cards." The process of ensuring that honesty in scoring prevailed throughout the game was a ritual not to be taken lightly. So it seemed to me on that fateful day of getting my first set of golf clubs that the foursome took an awful long time to settle up accounts for the honor of buying five cokes when my clubs were up there on the wall of the clubhouse gathering dust. Maybe even all being sold before I had a chance to pick out my set!

I knew every set of clubs for sale by heart. There were a couple of full sets of irons, all nine from three iron through nine iron, a putter and a wedge. There were a few more reduced sets—irons three, five, seven and nine along with a putter. And there were several sets of woods. Some were Wilson's, others Spaulding's. I had long ago cast my eyes on a reduced set of Wilson irons, figuring that a company with my name was bound to be good, although the Wilsons of Rolla had nothing in common with the Wilsons of the sporting goods company. All of those sets of clubs were hanging on the far side of the clubhouse, right opposite the front door entrance so that those who entered could not help but seeing what was available for purchase.

I followed Dad through a small shop door on the right hand side of the clubhouse. The wall just to the right of the door was covered with large postures of well known professionals. . .Bobby Jones, of course. . .Walter Hagen in his knickers. . .Sam Snead looking thoroughly relaxed on his way to another victory.

To the left of the door was a wood burning, potbellied stove for cool spring days but of little use during most of the hot, humid summer season. At the far end was the golf counter where Walter held forth. Walter was an institution. He had been there from the beginning, way back, so rumor had it, to when the School of Mines officials first decided a golf course was an important part of the education of budding mining engineers.

I never saw Walter swing a golf club nor give an official golf lesson. I don't even think he played the game. But he seemed to know a lot about the game, especially when it came time for the Missouri State Amateur Tournament. He knew every local player by name and those who had made it to the Missouri State tournament by every score on every round. Not that this was such a major task for there were only two during my day—Ken Lanning and Gene Sally. Both were local heroes. They were as close as Rolla came to having "professional athletes" of any sort. And both were more than willing to help out Rolla youngsters improve their game once they had learned the basics from their dads. I hoped to become one of those. But first I had to select my set of irons and woods.

That day, my sights were set on a shiny set of reduced Wilson irons. I waited for Dad to tell Walter to take it down from the shelf and hand it over to its new and rightful owner.

"Walter, where you got that barrel of old used clubs," I heard Dad say.

"Over there in the far corner by the potbellied stove, J.R. Why? You going to trade in that set of yours?"

"Nope. Going to keep mine. But I need to pick out a couple of irons for my son to begin learning on," Dad answered.

I stood frozen in disbelief. A couple of used rusted irons from the barrel! No new shiny set of Wilson irons. What's going on? How am I going to become a great golfer, maybe the next Ken Lanning, learning on a mismatched set of old irons? But I was in no position to question the wisdom of Dad, nor that of Walter, as I soon learned.

"Good idea, J.R. Start him out with just a couple. Maybe a three iron and a seven iron along with a putter. He can learn to drive with a three iron and how to handle the seven iron. Once he's got those under control we can start adding, say a five iron and a nine iron."

"He's left-handed," Dad stated matter-of-factly to Walter. "Don't suppose you got any left handed clubs in that barrel?"

"Nope. I don't. But that doesn't matter. Teach him to swing right-handed. He'll be a better golfer as a result. I've seen a goodly number of left-handers in my day swinging a club right handed and they do very well. Seems the left hand gives them more strength on the follow-through."

And with that Dad and Walter picked out a three iron and a seven iron and a putter, which became my full set of clubs for that first summer of learning the game of golf. No need to worry about carrying a bag when I could easily clutch my three clubs in my hand as I strode up and down the fairways. Nor did I need a bag to carry golf balls since I was given a new box of three and told to find lost balls in the rough from other players to supplement the three which I carried stuffed in the back rear pocket of my blue jeans.

"Grab a handful of tees out of the jar there and stuff them in your other pocket," Walter said to me to complete my new golf set. "When you break one just look around the tee for replacements. We got a lot of old salts out there who don't bother to pick up tees when they drive, so you won't have any problem keeping yourself in tees."

Fully armed with three used, mismatched clubs, a pocket of three new golf balls on one side and a handful of wooden tees in a pocket on the other side of my jeans, I headed out with Dad to the "driving range" to begin to learn the basics. The driving range was nothing more than the bare ground out back of the clubhouse where a couple of tractors and a mower were parked. About a hundred yards beyond the tractors and the mower a flag had been driven into the ground to signal a green.

I was instructed by Dad in how to grasp the three iron—hook the little finger of my right hand over the second finger of my left hand, firmly grasp the club a few inches below the top, keep my eyes riveted on a make-believe ball sitting on top of a wooden tee. Next, keep my left arm straight as I swung slowly backward, bending my wrists in a cocked position, elevating the club well beyond my back, then swing through with a smooth and graceful swoop as I connected with the ball and drove it long and straight towards the flag.

After a few dozen practice swings I was ready for the real thing, or so I thought. Puffing out my chest and striding forward with my eyes peering far out into the distance, I imagined my ball sailing far over those tractors and the mower and coming to rest at the base of the flag looming out there on the horizon. I carefully placed my tee and ball into the bare ground at my feet, took a step backward, positioned my feet square to the ball and tee and took careful aim. What happened from the backswing to the follow through was a mystery to me. I swung with every ounce of strength I had and ended up with the three iron pointed straight down the path in line with the flag looming out there in the far distance. Unfortunately my ball only managed to drib-ble its way about ten feet from the tee and sit there grinning back at me, or so it seemed. I looked back at Dad with one of those what went wrong looks.

"Well, Pete," he finally said. "You swung way too hard. That's not a baseball down there you're trying to pound out into left field. You looked up, your backswing was too shallow, and your follow through too fast. You topped the ball and probably sliced it. This game of golf is not so easy, is it?"

Dad and I spent the rest of that summer learning how to slow down my swing and all the other intricacies that I was being taught in order to propel what looked like a simple task of getting a little ball from one point of ground to a hole in another part of ground. It seemed to me that there was an awful lot to learn to this game.

The next summer my set of clubs was supplemented with a five iron and a nine iron and a three wood. These required additional mastery. And the following Christmas I finally got a full set of Wilson irons, all nine, and a full set of Wilson woods, all three. By the end of my third summer, now toting my own bag full of irons and woods up and down the fairways of the School of Mines course, I had become fairly proficient in getting the little white golf ball from one hole in the ground to another hole in the ground. But I was playing far more than just on a Sunday afternoon. I was playing every day when chores and studies and other matters had been put to rest.

By then I had found my own twosome or foursome of guys my age who were also learning to master the game. We played by the local rules—prox, putts, lowball and low total. We also fashioned rules that seemed essential on the hard baked clay course with greens made of oiled sand. This was not a fancy country club course that the powers to be up at the School of Mines had built, but a hard nosed sand lot course that was prevalent throughout most of rural Missouri at the time, and especially rural Missouri down in the Ozarks. Sand greens soaked in oil were far cheaper to maintain that the closely cropped grass greens of the fancy country clubs in St. Louis and Kansas City. Water was not to be wasted on keeping fairways supple and green during the long hot summer days. Let nature take its course. And that meant that as the hot summer season progressed the supple and green fairways of spring gave way to hard baked, brown runways of late summer.

We learned to drive our balls low and hard, knowing that they would then roll another fifty or so yards after gliding to the hard surface a hundred or so yards down field. We learned to pitch our shots to the green pin high, knowing that wherever the ball landed on the oily sand it would stick. No need to worry about pitching to the green and the ensuing roll towards the pin. Go straight for the pin and stick it. Putting was no big deal. Those oiled sand greens were as flat as a pancake and one simply smoothed a path down the sand from where his ball landed to the hole. We did enforce a rule that one had to putt down the middle of the raked path towards the hole. It wasn't cricket to line the ball up along one side of the path and simply putt down the line to the hole.

Also, we allowed each other to move the ball one club head from where it landed to get a better lie. This was necessary since the fairways by the middle of the summer were little more than tuffs of dried grass sticking up out of hard red clay dirt. So we could lift our ball to the closest tuff of grass to get a better lie. But once in the rough, which was nothing more than blackberry brambles, tall native grasses, dried out milkweed pods and wild sassafras bushes all tangled up in a harsh undergrowth, we had to hack our way out with no improvement in lie.

We soon began to bend those rules a little. The club head length was expanded to a foot or two. A missed swing or two in the rough could be discounted. Strokes could be shaved here and there so long as one did not get caught. Our recorded scores began to plummet as a result. Each score was dutifully recorded on a big score sheet that Walter kept posted on the outside of the clubhouse, just to the left of the shop door. Ken Lanning and Gene Sally were always listed at the very top. That was to be expected from the two "local pros." And they were followed by a handful of Rolla males who were good golfers in their own right, a little shy of being classified as "local pros" but certainly well able to get around the course at a fast clip. Then there were those of us who were of the younger set, myself included, who were rapidly moving up the ladder of local rankings and local fame.

"J.R., that son of yours is really becoming a good golfer. Maybe you aren't working him hard enough."

"Hey, J.R., I see from the scoreboard that that son of yours is beating the socks off you now."

"Well, J.R., you got another Ken Lanning in the making?"

And so it was that Dad said to me one day. . . "Pete, let's go out and have a game, just the two of us. Maybe I can pick up a pointer or two now that you have made so much progress with your buddies."

We teed off at one. Dad and I both shot a par four. No big deal. Hole two. Another par for each of us. Hole three. I went one up. And then hole four. Disaster struck. I drove into the rough, missed a couple of swings before I had punched back out onto the fairway and landed in a bare spot a long way from a club head of turf. I reached down and moved my ball a couple of feet to a good piece of turf.

Drove to the green. Putted out in two. Then reported to Dad that I had shot five, one over par. Dad didn't say anything. He just wrote down a five on the score card opposite my name and walked his way to the next tee. It was a short par three which we both made. And then tee six. A long par five, dogleg to the left past several large oaks looming down the fairway at the point of the dogleg. I drove to clear the dogleg, hit one of those oaks square, and lost sight of where my ball landed. Dad took a more cautious route down the middle of the fairway. His ball was fully visible right in the middle. Mine was somewhere lost in brush under the oaks. Never did find it, but I quickly dropped a ball where I would have liked to have found it and made a nice drive up towards the green. Again, I reported my score, minus a lost ball, and Dad again dutifully recorded it. We both putted out. And then Dad turned to me and quietly said:

"Pete, why don't we just sit down for a minute to rest at the next tee before continuing? I'm feeling a little weary in this hot weather."

"O.K." I answered.

We sat down on the wooden bench right behind the tee—Dad at one end of the bench and me at the other. Neither of us said anything. An eerie feeling soon enveloped me. Something wasn't right. Dad was unusually quiet. Something must be troubling him, I thought to myself.

"Pete," he quietly broke the silence. "I couldn't help but notice your game today. You haven't been shooting straight with me."

"What do you mean, Dad?" I responded, perplexed about what he was talking about. I had been playing the game I played with my buddies and it all seemed straight to me. I couldn't image what bugged him. But he soon let me know.

"Pete, I saw you take a couple of missed swings back on four. Then you dropped a ball in the oaks for the one you lost. And then you moved your ball several feet to get a better lie. All of these things are little things. But they do count in the long run."

"I don't understand what you're getting at." I abruptly responded. "We're just playing a game of golf, you know."

"I know. But it's more than just a game of golf. It really bothers me that you are learning to cut corners. The score doesn't mean a thing to me. I know you can beat me. You can beat a lot of others, as well. But you're not being truthful to yourself and to me and to others. You aren't playing the game of golf. You are playing the game of cutting corners. Winning isn't everything. How you win is. If you start cutting corners in golf you will soon cut corners in other things. You've got to shoot straight in everything you do. . .golf. . .tests in school. . .on the job. . .with the family. . .everything."

Dad paused, staring straight ahead down the fairway. I sat still, staring down at my feet. I didn't know what to say. All of a sudden my desire to win, and my pride in moving up the master scoring list on the clubhouse wall, seemed sullied and dirty. I squirmed deep down inside. I had been playing by a set of rules that made sense to me and my buddies, but clearly didn't make sense to Dad.

"Pete," Dad said ever more slowly. "I have my values and you have got to develop your own set. Mine may not be yours. But I think mine work, at least for the world I have lived in. Honesty is worth a lot in my world. Your world may be different. But doing what is right and standing up for what is right are values that I hope you will embrace as well. Doing the right thing will not always come easily. There are times when you will want to fudge the truth a little, cut corners, not shoot straight. I hope you won't. But you have to decide how you want to live your life. I just know how I have chosen to live my life. The game of golf is a lot more than simply shooting a low score and winning. The game of golf is about life itself."

RITES OF
PASSAGE

john oliver wilson

BIRD DOGS, QUAIL. . .AND CHORES!

IT WAS A COLD DAY IN EARLY NOVEMBER and Dad and I were riding back from a day in the cornfields hunting quail. I was just a little north of nine at the time and was about to begin my journey from boyhood to manhood. If I had known what was in store on this journey I might have elected to remain a boy for the rest of my life. But I really didn't have much choice in the matter, either biologically or in the eyes of my dad.

To Dad's way of thinking there were certain passages that every young boy must go through in order to make his mark on the world. As I soon found out he called this process "learning how to take responsibility for yourself." After encountering the first couple of passages, I put a little different slant on the word "responsibility."

It seemed to me that Dad was simply passing on from one generation to the next, me being the next, what his dad had passed on to him: The infinite wisdom of raising young boys in the Midwest. To wit: To keep your young son from getting into trouble, simply work him to death! But that is getting a little ahead of my story and really doesn't do full justice to the whole ordeal of rites of passage.

We had been out at Bobby Jack's farm. Bobby Jack and I were classmates and his dad and mine had shaken hands a few times when my dad was in the business of extending farm credit. Dad was now in business for himself, selling Dodge trucks and cars to all those farmers with whom he had shaken hands in the past. Dad had taken me along with him to Bobby Jack's to walk the fields once again under the pretext of hunting quail.

Quail are hard little creatures to come by. They simply don't seem to want to cooperate when they find themselves on the wrong end of a bird dog and a shotgun. So we didn't have many quail to show for our efforts. But we had given Cocoa a good workout.

Cocoa was our bird dog, and my best and closest friend. I had never known life without Cocoa. As you might gather from his name his coloring was brown with white splotches thrown in, for relief. He was considered by the locals as one of the best bird dogs in the county. Indeed, Dad had turned down an offer to sell him for $100 which was big money in those days. But like all bird dogs Cocoa had to have his day in the field. This is really what we were all about that day.

The two dads and Bobby Jack and I spent the day striding up and down the stubble of the cornfield with Cocoa out front where he could ferret out the quail. Once the scent hit his nose he was expected to freeze in the traditional point position. But it had been awhile since Cocoa had exercised his God-given talents, and on the first scent he broke point. With that Dad strode forward about as mad and determined as I had ever seen him. He grabbed Cocoa by the collar, smacked him across the nose and ordered him back into freeze position. I observed this event in horror. Then I ran forward and threw my arms around Cocoa's neck and nuzzled his head next to mine for comfort for both of us. With that Dad simply said: "Pete, it's all right. I didn't hurt him. He just has to learn discipline and responsibility."

I guess that is why I was about to receive my first instructions in responsibility as Dad and I bounded our way back to Rolla in the front end of the Dodge pickup, with Cocoa tied up behind in the bed. Dad obviously had responsibility on his mind. The lesson went something like this.

"Pete, you're getting to be a young man these days, and there are certain things a young man must learn. You have to learn how to take care of yourself and your mother and your sisters. Now that we have moved to the big house we have a lot of work to do. You and I will be spending a lot of time together and I need your help. So when we get home we'll sit down and work out a list of chores for you. It won't interfere with your school work or play. But we all have to learn how to take responsibility. Okay?"

I didn't view okay as an open question, which I could counter. It seemed, even at my tender age at the time, as simply closure to a point of fact. So, I remained quiet, somewhat nervous in anticipation of just what was involved in "chores." I didn't have to wait long.

Dad quickly laid down a list. Get up every morning, go down to the kitchen and start the fire in the stove so that the kitchen is warm and the stove is heated up when your mother comes down to cook breakfast. Keep the wood box filed with kindling. Fill the coal hopper down in the cellar every afternoon after you get home from school, and check the gauges of the furnace to make sure water pressure into the furnace is alright. Help me clean up the land of all the brambles and vines and turn it into a real yard. Clean out Cocoa's doghouse every day and put in fresh straw for him to sleep on.

The last of this list didn't seem like a chore. Unbeknownst to Dad, I was already doing this. The doghouse was out behind the garage and Cocoa and I had long before reached an agreement on a joint sharing of his turf. I found it a great hiding place, a place where I could crawl in with Cocoa and feel far removed from parents and sisters and all those outside intrusions on a young boy's inner life. So I had been keeping the doghouse clean for some time as a matter of course.

But those other chores were a different matter! As we bounded our way through the outskirts of Rolla headed for home, I gave the issue of chores a pretty deep thought. And the more I thought, the more I became a little concerned about what was in store in this learning to take responsibility.

"Dad, now that list of chores. Why don't we just replace a few of those chores with some others, such as hunting quail and working Cocoa?"

Dad didn't say anything. He just kept staring straight ahead, driving the pickup with Cocoa tied up in back. Maybe he didn't hear me, I thought to myself. Or maybe he isn't going to answer. But a few minute later, he let me know in no uncertain terms that doing chores was a necessary right of passage for young boys, and for me in particular.

Oh, well. I guess Cocoa and I could work this out in his home behind the shed. But I wondered to myself, is there any way I could teach a bird dog with God-given talents how to chop wood and fill the coal hopper?

JOE WEIDER AND HIS BARBELLS

I WAS NOT THE PUGILISTIC TYPE. I NEVER sought out fights on the playground. Indeed, I went out of my way to avoid fights. But in a small rural town in the Ozarks, and I assume it is true in any town or city, or wherever, playground fights are a fact of growing up. Something like a right of passage. So I was not able to avoid the inevitable. The time came when I would have to face up to defending my rights. I had to square off against a Mickey, or a Leroy, or some other classmate who had mastered the art of playground fist-a-cuffs. I always knew that day would come. One of the local toughs would catch me unawares on my way to East Elementary School.

Unfortunately, it was not Mickey or Leroy who first caught me unawares and unprepared. It was Joyce. A girl no less! The height of complete disgrace. Joyce lived in a small white shingle house that fronted just off the sidewalk on East Elm Street, a short cut-through street from my home on Salem Avenue to East Elementary School. I had walked past Joyce's house every day for nearly two years without any thought of fear or foreboding. Sometimes, as I was passing by, she would come swinging down from her porch steps, her blond hair waving in the breeze and her blue eyes blazing and we would walk to school together.

She was what you might call a "tomboy" which meant that she could match any of us boys on the softball diamond and generally out hit and outfield most of us, me included.

I had first met Joyce in the third grade and we were both now in Mrs. Jones fourth grade class. I liked Joyce. I always thought she was what today we'd call a "liberated woman."

It was one of those warm spring days when you could smell the earth beginning to stir. Daffodils were showing their yellow and white faces, announcing the end of winter and the beginning of spring. A warm breeze was in the air and I was feeling very good about myself, and life in general. Joyce came swinging down the front porch steps. I paused waiting for her to join me, little prepared for what was about to occur. I don't know to this day what set Joyce off. Maybe she had a fight with her mother. Or, maybe she wasn't feeling too good, or had just woken up on the wrong side of the bed that morning. But she certainly was not in the spring mood. No daffodils in her life that morning.

All I knew was that we were soon engaged in a roaring argument. And the next thing I knew is that she hit me square in the face with a very solid straight with her right fist. I grabbed for my face. She landed a beautiful left hook and followed it up with another right. By then I was on the ground. It was over in a flash. I can still see Joyce in my mind turning her back and heading down the street to East Elementary School leaving me where I lay. I slunk into class a few minutes later avoiding any eye contract with Joyce or anyone else. It was a miserable day. I knew that I had to do something to regain my male self-confidence.

I found the answer later that night while flipping through the pages of my latest *Boy's Life*. An ad for Joe Weider and Company showed two scenes. In the first, a little skinny kid on the beach was having sand kicked into his face by a big bully. And, in the second, the same skinny kid not looking so skinny now as he sported big bulging biceps and a massive muscular chest, was pounding the big bully into the sand. The pictures were given the title: Before and After. The ad promised that for $49.99 you could get a complete set of barbells and weights with ropes and pulleys and headgear and body building course instructions that were "guaranteed" to turn you from "before" to "after" in a matter of a few months of 30 minute workouts, three times a week.

I cleaned out my savings, bought a money order from the Rolla National Bank for $49.99 plus mailing costs of $9.99 made out to Joe Weider and Company. And, I began my wait. One week passed. No barbells. Two weeks passed. Still no barbells. Week three and week four came and went. I was beginning to think that I had been taken.

School was now out for summer vacation. I was off on my lawn mowing business. I had just finished mowing Mrs. Walker's yard across the road, and was putting the mower back in the shed when sister Pat suddenly appeared in the doorway.

"Johnny, you better get around to the front porch on the double and see what has happened," she blurted out in a voice highly agitated.

"What happened?" I quickly asked.

"You'll see," was all I could get in reply.

I ran to the front of the house and bounded up on the porch. Right at the front door I found a big gaping hole in our porch. Lying on the ground sat a large box addressed to Mr. John O. Wilson, 611 Salem Avenue, Rolla, Missouri. The box had Joe Weider Barbells printed in large black letters on all sides. Clearly, the mailman had dropped the box at our front door not knowing that the wooden deck was rotten, and Dad had it on his "to-do" list to replace it with a concrete one. Unfortunately, the to-do list had yet to be done, and so I stood there staring down at my newly arrived barbells but faced with the looming problem of how to explain this to Dad when he arrived home in a matter of a few hours.

I quickly opened the box, lifted out the barbells and weights and hid them away in the back shed. I then found a piece of plywood and carefully nailed it over the gaping hole on the porch floor. And then, I waited the inevitable, hoping Dad would come in through the back door which was his usual way of entering the house. But unfortunately, he took it is his mind on this particular night to come through the front door. It seemed to me sitting upstairs in my bedroom that it took him an awful long time to get through the door. But once inside I heard the "inevitable" begin to take shape.

"Honey Dear," he called out to Mother. "What's going on by the front door?"

"You better speak to your son," she replied. "He's upstairs in his bedroom."

"Pete, come on down. I need to talk to you."

With this summons I slowly descended the stairs putting the final touches on my defense. Dad was standing out on the porch looking down at the plywood I had carefully nailed over the gaping hole.

"What's this?" he asked.

"Well, Dad. It's like this," I began, pausing to give final shape to my story. "I knew that you wanted to replace the rotten deck but were just too busy to get it done. So I thought I would get started and we could work on it together."

I thought that was a pretty good story myself. But apparently Dad thought otherwise. He gave me one of those looks that tell all, which means he didn't believe one word of my story. He just gave the plywood a shove with his foot and the cover moved off the gaping hole. Then I realized why he had been so long in coming through the front door. He had gone to the shed to get a hammer and had removed the nails I had so carefully pounded in and examined the evidence.

"Now, Pete. You can do better than that. You would never have begun removing the deck up by the front door by pounding a hole through the floor. You would have started out at the edge of the porch, prying up the boards one at a time with a crowbar. So come clean. What's going on?"

I explained to Dad, "I want to get stronger and build up my body. I saw this ad for barbells in *Boy's Life*, I took my savings from lawn mowing and sent away for a set of barbells and weights. The mailman must have dropped the heavy box on the front porch not knowing that it was rotten. When I got home earlier today from mowing Mrs. Walker's lawn, Pat showed me what had happened. I covered up the hole with plywood so no one would fall through and hurt themselves."

I left out the bit about Joyce beating me up and causing me all this trouble to begin with.

"Why didn't you tell me this in the first place?" Dad asked.

"Well, I didn't know how you would feel about my ordering the barbells," I truthfully answered.

"I understand," Dad said. "Let's just sit down on the side of the porch and talk this through."

We sat down and Dad explained to me that I always needed to be truthful. It is a lot easier in the long run than trying to make up a story when the truth will come out anyway. That I agreed with. Then he said he understood my desire to develop my muscles and get stronger. That is a part of growing up. But there were many ways to develop my muscles, and he had one in mind. Not that this would interfere or take away from my pleasure in lifting weights and following the training program sent by Joe Weider. He had been giving some thought to the backyard, and how we could build it up and make it a real yard.

Our backyard, or I should say the land back of our house, fell off in a deep slant down towards a gully that led off into the woods. It wasn't really a backyard, and it was covered with briars and brambles. We hadn't cleaned it up yet like the front and side yards.

"So," Dad continued, "I think we should get some rocks or material that we could use to build up the back and stabilize the ground, and then fill it over with dirt. Then we can plant grass seed and have a real yard."

"But where will we get the rock and the men to build up the slant?" I asked. It was a delaying question for I already sensed the answer that was about to come.

"Well, that is where you come in," Dad began, "I saw the other day that they are ripping up the sidewalks over on 12th Street and pouring new sidewalks. So I have asked the town for the old concrete blocks. I thought that it would be good exercise for you to bust up those concrete blocks this summer and we could use that for fill. You will build up your muscles real fast."

About three days later, a big dump truck arrived and deposited a pile of large concrete blocks in our new backyard area. Dad arrived later that evening toting a newly purchased sledge hammer and goggles and proceeded to show me how to swing the sledge hammer using my weight and arms for leverage so to not hurt my back. The goggles were to keep concrete chips from hitting my eyes.

I looked over that great big pile of concrete. I hoisted the sledge hammer and felt its weight. I envisioned what it was going to be like on a hot summer morning pounding concrete. I peered down the gully and quickly realized that this was no easy task to be whipped out in a day or two. The better part of the summer was going to be spent breaking up concrete blocks, rolling them down into the gully to build up the ground more level, and then hauling dirt for fill, and eventually sowing grass seed.

This is not quite how I had envisioned I was going to spend my summer vacation. And I quickly made a promise to myself that next time I would be a little more careful about what I ordered from Joe Weider and Company.

THE MANLY ART
OF SELF-DEFENSE

CHRISTMAS WAS A SPECIAL TIME around our household. My sisters and I carefully leafed our way through the Sears catalogue and turned down pages and marked those items we especially wanted Santa Claus to bring that year. Then we would place the catalogue on the kitchen counter, in obvious view of Dad and Mother, expecting them to leaf through the catalogue on their own in search of ideas and stumble onto our well marked preferences.

Christmas of 1950 was no different. I had carefully marked camping equipment, for I was now a member of Boy Scout Troop 82. I wanted a new camping tent, a sleeping bag, air mattress, cook stove, hatchet, hiking boots, rain parka, and special cook kit of three nestled pots with lids. Quite an extensive list. But I figured that any three or four of the items would be doing well this Christmas and I could pick up the others the next go around.

That morning I bounded down the stairway, followed by my sisters, Pat and Kathy, to start the Christmas morning ritual. We weren't allowed to open our gifts until Dad and Mother were awake, dressed, and done their chores. It always seemed to us on Christmas morning that they took an inordinate amount of time to accomplish these tasks, just to harass the younger members of the family. But finally they appeared. And, one by one, we began to unwrap and share what we had received around the family circle.

As my turn came I began to add to my pile: new jeans, a couple of flannel shirts, some new books for my growing library, but no sleeping bag, air mattress, cook stove or anything else I had carefully marked in the Sears catalogue. But there was a big box sitting under the tree that had my name on it, and I hoped that this was my one great big special present from Santa. I waited anxiously until my turn came around once again. Surely that big box contained a sleeping bag or a camping tent. It was certainly big enough from all outward appearances.

Finally, it was my turn to open the special box. I pulled off the colored string with one mighty heave, tore off the wrappings, ripped open the top of the cardboard box, expecting my sleeping bag or camping tent and found. . .two sets of boxing gloves! Boxing gloves?

"Gee, Dad and Mom, I had no idea. What a great surprise. Thank you for such a nice present. I never dreamed I would be getting boxing gloves for Christmas," I managed to blurt out, slowly expressing my thanks and trying to hide my disappointment.

"Well, Pete, if you hadn't been so hasty in getting the box open you might have noticed a note attached on top."

Now we were talking. Undoubtedly the note would tell me that the sleeping bag and tent were on backorder, and just didn't make it in time for Christmas. I quickly found the note among the crumpled paper, opened it and read silently to myself.

"Merry Christmas. To go along with the present six boxing lessons from George Christopher. Much love, Dad."

George Christopher owned and operated Christopher Jewelry Store on Pine Street. I had been by his store many times in my wanderings up and down Pine Street, always ducking it to say hello and look longingly at the watches he kept well displayed under the counter glass. I knew that Mr. Christopher, as I called him, had been a professional boxer in his youth, fighting somewhere back east as a light middle-weight. Never did know if he ever fought in Madison Square Garden, but that was the local lore, at least among the junior high set.

I never thought of myself as a boxer. Why had Dad come up with this surprise on Christmas of 1950? All of sudden a horrible thought raced through my mind as I sat there watching my sisters open their big gifts. I wondered if Dad somehow found out that Joyce had beaten the living daylights out of me and this was a rite of passage in learning the manly art of self defense!

It just wouldn't go down well at the local coffee gatherings of the elders for Dad to be kidded by his friends about his son being beaten up by a girl! And I was not about to raise the issue. It was better to simply express great thanks for the lessons and the boxing gloves, and get on with it. After all, learning how to box might not be such a bad idea.

Several weeks later I made my way down to Christopher Jewelry Store on Pine Street and approached Mr. Christopher with the card from my Christmas gift.

"I've been expecting you," Mr. Christopher warmly greeted me even before I had time to open my mouth. I guess I didn't need the Christmas card to remind him of the reason I was there.

"You ready to get started with your lessons?

"Yes, Sir."

"Well, can you come back this afternoon around four? I will close up early, and we can head to my house where I have rigged a boxing ring in the garage."

"Yes, Sir."

Mr. Christopher and I walked to his house, a few blocks from Pine Street, and entered his garage. He threw on the lights and I saw a boxing ring right in the middle, complete with stanchions at the four corners and nylon ropes all around. Whether it was official size or not I didn't know, having no idea what official size was, but it certainly looked big and foreboding and threatening to me.

"Strip down to your undershirt and come on in," Mr. Christopher ordered.

I noticed that he had removed his tie, loosened the collar of his shirt, rolled up his sleeves and was busy lacing on his boxing gloves. I had toted along both sets of my new gloves, not knowing whether he had any of his own or not. I should have known better. One obviously did not fight in Madison Square Garden, or where ever, and not have a few sets of gloves from the past around for old memory sake.

He showed me how to lace up my gloves firmly, then he landed a few hard lefts and rights into a punching bag that was hanging down in one corner of the ring to get the feel. I did the same although my punches seemed pretty pale and weak in comparison to the sharp snap of those of Mr. Christopher. It began to dawn on me that those sharp snaps on the punching bag were just a hint of what was going to soon happen to my head. It wasn't a happy thought to say the least.

Mr. Christopher did not begin by pounding my head into oblivion. He showed me how to square off, how to keep my hands high and cocked, and how to work my feet so as to keep moving around the ring and not just stand there flatfooted offering my opponent a sitting target. He then started to throw a few gentle punches my way, jabbing with his left and then following it up with various hooks and counterpunches with his right. My head remained safe and intact and the only punches I felt were a few to my stomach when I let my guard down. We worked out for about 30 minutes and by then I was huffing and puffing and gasping for breath. This boxing was tough stuff, even without having to worry about getting my head knocked off.

Week followed week, and the lessons gradually progressed from gentle counter punching to some real stuff. I took a few hard shots to the head, but nothing that was damaging. Mr. Christopher kept coaching me about the sport of boxing, emphasizing that it was not about beating the daylights out of your opponent. Bouts were won and lost on the points earned from landing clean punches, not about knocking out your opponent as fast as possible. That was for the pros.

Amateur boxing, at least as I was being taught by Mr. Christopher, was about style and speed and earning clean points. Not that this was akin to playing tiddlywinks. Boxing was an art of self defense, not to be taken lightly. I had to know how to defend myself against sandlot fighters who played by different rules, or even girls who knew how to handle their fists even though they had never been inside a boxing ring.

When the lessons with Mr. Christopher ended, I needed to find a willing opponent. Someone my age who would spar around with me on an equal basis, but who would not suddenly turn into a raging tiger and proceed to do serious damage to my head and or my body. I wanted to learn this sport, not become a punching bag for some sandlot toughie.

I hit upon the ideal opponent: Millard.

Millard and I were the closest of friends. I first met him in the second grade, and we soon realized we were cut from the same bolt of cloth. Millard had a vast array of interests—building timber forts in the woods behind his house, heading down his road with our .22's to target practice at tin cans and rats in the town dump, hiking through the Ozark hills and camping out at Piney River, working on math lessons and learning photography, and playing the trumpet. I had the same interests. We spent many a day roaming the hills, plotting our futures, or just having a good time growing up together. It seemed to me a perfect choice. I knew Millard would be willing to learn how to box with me.

Unfortunately, I overlooked one small detail in selecting Millard as my boxing partner. He was significantly bigger and stronger and more physically developed than I was. Millard could well defend himself, as I was soon to learn.

I shared with him some of what I had learned from Mr. Christopher—how to stand, how to dance around our make-believe ring, how to throw punches and how to block those punches. We laced on our gloves. Millard seemed to get the hang of boxing pretty fast. He squared away in front of me and then began to dance around to get the feel of moving about, and threw some shadow punches off to one side. Then he came back and squarely faced me and matter-of-factly stated:

"Let's give it a go."

"Right on," I responded, somewhat cocky.

I figured that with my "advance training" from Mr. Christopher, I would more than hold my own with Millard, at least for the time being. So I lashed out a couple of jabs. They landed on Millard's head, but didn't seem to make a dent. I then proceeded to dance around, flashing more jabs and a few counterpunches. It seemed to me a pretty good show. Then Millard let me know in no uncertain terms that boxing was not something to be taken lightly.

His eyes suddenly narrowed. His chest filled up with a big inhale. Suddenly he seemed twelve feet high. Then he fired a right hand, hitting me square in the head and sent me reeling off my feet and square onto my backside. I had never felt anything like that from Mr. Christopher, or Joyce, or anyone else for that matter! The room spun around in my head. I gasped for breath. Millard immediately sat down beside me and asked if I was okay.

"Yep," I finally was able to mutter. "But that was some punch you just hit me with."

Millard was distraught.

"I really didn't mean to hurt you. I just threw what I thought was a good solid punch like you told me to do."

"Yeah, it was good and solid all right."

"Why don't we get our .22's and go do some shooting. I think we have done enough boxing for one day," Millard suggested.

"Good idea," I hastily answered.

As far as I was concerned we had done enough boxing, period. Next time, I thought, I'll be a little more careful about picking my boxing opponent—maybe sister Pat.

MICKEY AND HIS DRIVING MACHINE

D AD VIEWED LEARNING TO DRIVE AS LITTLE more than a rite of
passage. Driving was a necessary skill, much the same as learning how to type, or how to budget. I needed to know how to drive to
get around in the world.

My high school classmates had other ideas. Driving was freedom!
It was access to Route 66 and to parking and petting. It represented
the final break with the confining boundaries of home and Rolla.

I was caught somewhere between the two. I never was one who
desired to escape from home or Rolla. When I felt the boundaries of
either closing in on me I could easily escape on foot or bike to the
Ozark hills. So access to freedom was never a real issue. But I did view
learning to drive as something more than just a necessary skill to get
around in the world. I wanted my own car. The mechanics at Wilson-
Smith Motor Company and I had already conferred on my desire at
some length.

I knew that I could pick up an old used car for little cost and that
Shorty Johnson, the lead mechanic, would help me install a newly
rebuilt engine in whatever old car I could afford, to get it up to Rolla
standards. So the issue for me was to complete this right of passage as
soon as possible and get my driving license. The target date was May
22, 1954.

Unfortunately, Dad set about the task of meeting my target date in his usual methodical fashion. Sunday afternoons from 5:00 pm to 6:00 pm were set aside for driving lessons. I greatly appreciated the fact that he was willing to provide the training vehicle and spend an hour every Sunday evening teaching me how to drive. But it didn't take a mathematical genius to figure out that this rate of learning I would be an old man of eighteen before I ever completed this rite of passage. Something drastic had to be done to speed up the learning process.

Mickey was a classmate who lived across the street. And Mickey was worldly wise in ways that I could never hope to attain. So he came up with the logical solution to my problem.

Mickey had observed that my Dad always kept an idle car in the unattached garage behind our house. It was one of those farm type garages with a large wooden roll down door with just enough room for one car or pick-up truck and a dirt floor saturated with old oil spills. Off to the right was the work shed where Dad kept the mowers, rakes, hoes, picks, shovels and other tools of the trade. It had its own entrance door, so Dad rarely went into the auto storage part of the garage. He and Mother parked their cars outside at the far end of the yard. It was a perfect set up for the problem at hand. And I thought that Mickey came up with the perfect solution.

"All we have to do," Mickey informed me, "is to jack up the car and put four concrete cinder blocks at each corner to keep the wheels clear of the ground. Then, we simply connect a rubber hose to the exhaust and run it through a hole we can drill in the far side of the garage where it won't be seen. This is important so we don't asphyxiate ourselves. Then we are all set. I can start teaching you how to rev up the engine and shift gears."

I made fast progress in learning how to push the clutch down,

down shifting from first to second to third and back again, and then getting my foot back on the gas peddle to keep the engine roaring. Next, Mickey taught me how to shift into reverse and slowly keep the engine running as I backed up into a parking space, or simply for a turnaround.

Dad had no idea what was going on behind those closed doors of the garage, at least to my knowledge. However, I was a little concerned, when on one of our routine Sunday driving lessons he commented out the clear blue sky.

"My heavens, Pete, you are really catching onto this gear shifting fast."

My heart skipped a beat or two for I thought he might have stumbled into our training center by accident. He didn't press the issue. And I certainly let the discussion drop.

Things were going great guns and I had visions of getting my driving license on the exact day of my sixteenth birthday. I was dating Judy at the time and was already planning the drive across town in my newly rebuilt Plymouth coupe painted a bright metallic green. It was sitting, well covered up, in the back corner of the body shop of Wilson-Smith Motor Company, far out of sight of Dad, the owner. It was to be a movie date at the local drive-in and then a hot time parking down by the Gasconade River. Then, disaster struck!

Mickey and I were fast approaching the deadline date and were putting the final touches on the gear shifting business when we got into a heated discussion about stock car racing out at the local track. What would it be like to drive a stock car at a roaring speed around those dirt curves and into the high bank headed for the finish line? Would we have the guts to slug it out with other cars headed fast for the same lane? Our testosterone was working at full speed. We could hardly contain ourselves with the thought of the wind blowing in our face, our gloved hands gripping the wheel, with the roar of several hundred horsepower under our feet.

Mickey was at the wheel. To this day I am not sure what happened next. All I remember is the car suddenly dropping to the dirt floor in reverse and crashing into the garage door at the rear. Fortunately, we didn't crash our way through the door, but we sure as heck put a big bulge in it. The bottom half of the door was splintered and try as we might there was no way we could force the door up along its runners to conceal the damage at the top of the garage. I simply had to take my medicine when Dad came home that night. The end result was that I had to put off my driving test for six months while I repaired the damaged door, and did repentance.

Clearly, my driving trip to Judy's to show off my rebuilt Plymouth coupe had to be postponed. We celebrated my sixteenth birthday walking to the Uptown Theatre and stopping off at the Dairy Queen on our walk back home. So much for my visions of a drive-in movie and then a hot parking date down by the Gasconade River.

THIS ONE AIN'T GOING
TO BE EASY

"THIS ONE AIN'T GOING TO BE EASY," muttered Ike Skelton, as much to himself as to Charlie and me sitting next to him in the cab of his Ford pickup. We were driving south on Route 63 down towards Licking, headed to do another "buryin'" as Ike put it to me when he called a couple of days before.

Ike had served in World War II, as had Charlie. Now Ike was commander of American Legion Post 81 in Rolla, and doing another burying meant someone died who had served in the Army or Navy or Marines, and the family had requested a military service at graveside. Having done my first graveside duty when I helped bury Mr. Walrath, I was quickly adopted by the Post as the resident, and only bugler for taps. I guess I had blown taps at fifty or sixty buryings. I stopped counting after the first dozen or so, but it seemed to me that I was on call about every few weeks, for the hills around Rolla were full of men who had gone off to fight for their country. They all seemed to want to meet their Maker with the help of a military escort.

Most of the services were in the Rolla Cemetery, but a goodly number were in cemeteries tucked back in the hills all around Rolla. I had been to any number of country churches with the graveyard out back and an old buggy tie bar out front. Today, we were headed to Bear Hollow Baptist Church way back in the hills south of Rolla on an old rural route some twenty or so miles as the crow flies off Route 63.

"How's that?" questioned Charlie to Ike's mutterings.

"Well, I've known Bobby Turner since he was a kid," answered Ike. The truth was that Ike had known every one he helped bury since they were kids. But this one seemed to be different.

"Bobby comes from a good line. There are a whole passel of Turners throughout the hills around here. Bobby was one of the better ones. He went off to war before he could shave, landed at Normandy, and fought all the way across France and into Germany. Never even took one bullet. And then this."

This was a truck accident. Bobby had been driving into town when he came barreling around a tight turn on the route to 63 and saw a slow moving hay wagon directly in his path. Rather than plowing into the hay wagon and killing the young kid on the tractor, Bobby had taken to the ditch. Unfortunately, he hit a large oak and was thrown from the truck. The coroner said he must have hit his head on a rock, for his head was crushed in. He died immediately. "He didn't suffer none," the corner consoled the family.

It was a warm spring day. After the church service and burial out back, there was going to be a potluck supper on the church grounds. Ike and Charlie and I were looking forward to a real old-fashioned rural burial. No quick trip following the hearse out to the gravesite. No fast condolences to the family after folding of the American flag covering the casket and giving it to the widow or mother seated next to the grave in a metal folding chair. This was going to be the real thing.

A local Baptist minister who had heard the call when he was about my age, and learned his gospels straight from the Good Book, was slated to do the service, so we had been told. Here was a preacher who could do battle with Satan directly from the pulpit without the benefit of any fancy seminary training. We knew it was going to a long afternoon of prayers, and gospels, and eulogies, and words of faith and hope. A self-taught Baptist preacher didn't let an opportunity like this slip by any too fast, especially when burying one of the Turner tribe.

We pulled up in front of the church and took our place alongside a number of other Ford, Chevy, and Dodge pickups. There were even a few horse drawn buggies hitched to the old tie bar off to the side near the woods. The family and locals were all milling around just outside the entrance to the church. It was the typical backwoods church— whitewashed, long and rectangular, steps leading directly up from the front grounds to the sanctuary, wooden pews on the left and right, aisle running straight down to the chancel, and the pulpit off to the left.

The cemetery was located behind the church. To the right of the church were the picnic grounds where long flat boards had been placed on top of wooden sawhorses to serve as tables for the potluck supper. Blue and white checkered oil cloth had already been spread over the boards, and old wooden folding chairs had been placed up and down each side of the tables. Covered dishes of food were already in place, covered with dishcloths to keep the flies away until time to eat. The sign out front read: Bear Hollow Baptist Church, Founded: 1873. Clearly, these grounds had witnessed a goodly number of burials and potluck meals over the years. Bobby Turner was going to be in good company.

I looked around at the crowd. These were hard working folk, raw boned, weather worn, honest open faces, now dressed up in their Sunday best. I ambled my way into the crowd of locals, waiting for the movement into the church for the service. They nodded their heads and smiled a greeting, the Ozark way of welcoming strangers without making me feel out of place. I felt at home among these people, even though I was from the "big town of Rolla" and this was backwoods country.

In the front of the crowd stood a young woman dressed in black, who looked to be in her mid-twenties. She was holding the hand of a young blond-headed girl of about five or six. Next to the girl stood a flaxen-haired boy, a couple of years older. The young woman was Jamie Turner, widow of Bobby, and mother to their two young children. They were a good-looking family. Bobby Turner must have been a handsome man. He was only 29 when he died. To leave behind such a young family seemed a great tragedy.

I found myself looking at Jamie and wondering what was going to become of her. Her blond hair was pulled back in a tight bun, revealing an intelligent looking and very attractive face. Her black dress covered a slim and well-built figure. Undoubtedly, she would remarry. She would quickly catch the eye of some young buck, just as she had caught my eye. And then I suddenly pulled back to the present. I felt my face redden with embarrassment. I hoped that no one in the crowd could read my mind. How could I be thinking such thoughts when we had yet to put Bobby Turner to rest.

The crowd headed up the steps into the church, as if answering an unheard call to service. I waited behind. Then took a seat in a back pew knowing that I needed to exit as soon as the service was over so I could warm up my trumpet and get located in the woods near the gravesite. I wanted the taps to come from the woods and echo out over the surrounding hills.

We sang "Nearer My God to Thee," and then the preacher opened with a long winded prayer asking the Good Lord to welcome faithful servant Robert Jackson Turner, recently deceased on earth, but now at home in the one true home that awaits us all when our turn comes, and asking of the Good Lord peace and understanding for Jamison Ruth Turner, widow of the recently deceased, who knows that she will eventually be reunited with her beloved Bobby in the hereafter, then calling upon all so gathered to keep alive in our hearts and minds the blessed memory of Robert Jackson Turner, who was taken from our midst at the prime of his life on earth, but the ways of the Lord are mysterious and unfathomable, and we must keep the faith. Amen.

Ike was right. It was going to be a long afternoon for clearly our self-taught Baptist preacher was just warming up to his task. We were just past the first hymn and the opening prayer, and already half an hour had slipped by. I settled back in my pew and let my mind wander. This time, not about the tragic death of Bobby Turner and the future of Jamie Turner, but about what was in store for me.

When would I find my own Jamie? Would she be slim and attractive, and have an intelligent face? Would I be blessed with healthy and intelligent kids, maybe a boy and a girl? But first would I have to go off to war like Ike and Charlie and Bobby? Suddenly, this thought swooped down on me. Never before had I given the military much consideration.

I knew that I would have to register for the draft. But that seemed so far in the future that it had never entered my thoughts. I was too busy growing up. But now it seemed that I was not that far behind Bobby Turner. Would I be drafted in a couple of years and find myself in basic training down at Fort Leonard Wood? Was the Army in my future? Life was suddenly getting to be pretty serious business. A little too serious.

john oliver wilson

MEN, MACHINES
AND DREAMS

john oliver wilson

WILSON-SMITH MOTOR COMPANY

WILSON-SMITH MOTOR COMPANY was headquartered at 216 West 7th Street, just one block west of Pine Street. John R. Wilson was principal owner and head front-end alignment mechanic. This is where the Wilson came from in the company name. Alfred Smith, long-time friend of the family, was part owner and head of sales and marketing. This is where the Smith came from in the company name. Wilson-Smith Motor Company was in the business of selling and keeping in running order Dodge and Plymouth automobiles and Dodge trucks.

The company was founded in 1946. Dad had been offered a position in the regional office of Production Credit of the U.S. Department of Agriculture in St. Louis. However, Dad never felt comfortable in big cities, and the thought of leaving Rolla for the post-war booming suburbs of St. Louis was not in the cards. So he resigned from government service and went into business selling automobiles and trucks to the many farmers he had come to know throughout the Ozarks.

Selling automobiles and trucks was easy business in the post-World War II years. In fact, there was no selling involved, for the demand was far greater than the supply. The major activity of Wilson-Smith Motor Company, in those years, was to maintain fair and honest lists of those wanting vehicles and to ensure that after a wait of six to nine months those first on the list were honored. Being fair and honest was not an easy task, for additional money was readily offered to move higher on the list, particularly by non-locals who would come in from as far away as Chicago to buy scarce automobiles. There was also a booming business in buying automobiles at fair prices in the Midwest and driving them to California where they could be sold for many hundred dollars more.

To ensure that none of the vehicles sold by Wilson-Smith Motor Company ended up in California, Dad would deliver the long-awaited automobiles and trucks himself. He would usually take me along on these deliveries. I would first help him clean up and polish the new vehicles. Then the two of us would head out some country road to the lucky farmer and his family. I always liked these trips. Dad would get an honest shake of the hand from the new owner, and I would get a good farm dinner.

I pretty well knew my way around Wilson-Smith Motor Company before I found myself officially on the payroll. I ended up on the payroll when I decided to make a major change in my career direction. It was 1950, and I was twelve at the time. I had been in the lawn mowing business for two years, and was now ready to move on to bigger and better things.

Mowing lawns was all right so long as I was in East Elementary School. But, once I matriculated from the sixth grade and moved to Rolla Junior High School, I felt that mowing lawns was somewhat beneath my dignity. The truth of the matter was that mowing lawns in the Ozark summers was hot and humid work, a hard way to make a living. So when the summer season drew to a close, I announced to Dad that I was going to look for other employment for the next summer. That I had given the matter much careful thought and had come to the conclusion that I needed to take the next nine months off to recover from my stressful work experience, and decide what I was going to do next with my work life.

Dad had other ideas. Idleness was not part of his plan for keeping a young growing son out of trouble, and on the right path to becoming a productive member of society. This was especially true for a young son who was approaching the teenage years, and showing increasing interest in the opposite sex, and entering junior high school where all kinds of potential trouble were lurking.

"Pete, why don't you come down to the office and let's talk this over," Dad popped out over the dinner table one evening in late August.

Now, this was a new slant. I had never been asked to "come down to the office," nor was I sure what he meant by "office." But, I assumed he meant corporate headquarters of Wilson-Smith Motor Company. That night, as I lay in bed and pondered my future, I grew increasingly uneasy about my upcoming meeting at the office. I came to the conclusion that it was best to get the office discussion out of the way as fast as possible. So the next morning I hopped on my bike and peddled my way down to 7th and Pine. Dad was sitting at his desk going through some paperwork when I knocked on the open door to get his attention.

"Come on in, Pete, and sit down," he said motioning to a chair beside his desk. "I have been giving some thought to your desire for a change in work, and have a proposal for you to consider. John Goggin has been doing the clean up work around the back room for the past several years, but John is getting up in years and he needs to devote his full attention to running the parts department. This is something you might want to consider taking on, cleaning up the back room.

John Goggin had been with Dad from the beginning when he first started the motor company. Mr. Goggin, as I called him, was in his mid-seventies, and lived with his wife, Ellie, out west of town in a small white frame house that sat up on a hill above the highway. He and Ellie had raised their family in Rolla, but their children had long ago moved elsewhere. Now John and Ellie kept pretty much to themselves, quietly enjoying the twilight years of their long life together.

"Old Man Goggin," as he was known to the locals, left his small white frame house at 5:30 a.m. each morning of the week, with the exception of Sunday, and walked the mile and a half to the Wilson-Smith Motor Company. He arrived around 6:15 a.m. or 6:30 a.m., depending on how much pep he had that particular day, unlocked the front door, turned on the lights, ambled back to the mechanics area and selected a broom with which he would sweep up the debris from the previous day's work. In winter months, he filled the coal hopper and stoked up the large boiler, and turned on the fans, forcing the heated air though big ducts covering the ceiling. When the mechanics arrived at 7:30 a.m. to begin the day, they wanted their "office" to be warm and toasty.

When Mr. Goggin finished his back room work he moved to the front office where the parts department was located. For the remainder of the work day he would look up parts numbers in the large MoPar Parts manuals on top of the counter that served to separate the offices of the mechanics from the parts department. He would then locate the parts in various bins and shelves where gaskets, carburetors, mufflers, tailpipes, brake linings, fuel pumps, pistons and even engine heads were inventoried.

At noon, Mr. Goggin walked the mile and a half back to his small white frame house where Ellie had a lunch of soup and sandwich waiting for him. By 2:00 pm he was back at 7th and Pine. At 6:30 pm he checked the back room to make sure that everything was in order, banked the furnace for the evening, turned off the lights, locked up Wilson-Smith Motor Company, and walked his way back to Ellie and his small white frame house.

Dad offered me the job of cleaning up the mechanics area and caring for the furnace in winter months that Mr. Goggin had long done. The clean-up work was laid out as removing all oil and grease areas on the floor with a special sawdust absorbing mixture, and sweeping up the sawdust mixture and all other debris left on the floor from the previous day's work. Then I was to clean the work benches of the mechanics, carefully placing tools in each mechanic's chest and aligning auto jacks, auto stands, cleaning rags, lighting cords, and all other special equipment, just as each mechanic desired. Since all four mechanics employed at Wilson-Smith Motor Company were strong individualists, I needed to learn how each of them wanted their "offices" cleaned and maintained.

I was to arrive at work each morning at 6:15 a.m., in time to meet Mr. Goggin, who would unlock the premises for the day. If I worked diligently and efficiently, I would be done by 8:00 a.m. and have time to clean up and ride my bike to school for the beginning class, at 8:30 a.m.. For this I would be paid a starting rate of $1.00 per day, but on Saturdays I could earn more by cleaning and polishing the cars and trucks waiting for delivery to new owners. I thought this was a great new opportunity.

Mother thought otherwise. That night she was unusually quiet over dinner. As soon as the dishes were cleared, she turned to Dad and announced in her best debater tone:

"John, you and I need to have a private discussion. Now!"

"Yes, Honey Dear," Dad responded.

He generally called Mother "Honey Dear," especially when she got her dander up and began to move into her debating mode. My sisters and I knew the warning signs from past encounters, so we quickly excused ourselves from the table and made a hasty retreat upstairs. However, I sensed this discussion concerned my immediate future, so I tucked myself out of sight at the bottom of the stairs, but within hearing range of the kitchen table.

"John, I know what your have offered our son, and I don't like it a bit. He will have to get up every morning at 5:30 a.m., fix his own breakfast, and ride his bike in the dark and cold down to the garage. There he will be exposed to all kinds of tough language and rude behavior. I know your mechanics are good men, but that is no environment for a twelve-year-old. He is still growing and he needs his sleep. Getting up so early in the morning, and working two hours before school begins, is not good. He has his music. He is beginning to develop as a good debater. He needs to keep his grades up. And you continue to work him around the house. What are you trying to do? Kill him!"

"Now, Honey Dear, I hear you. You know that I have Pete's best interest at heart. I would never do anything to set him back. But I think he can handle it. It will be good for him to learn the ways of business. I will keep a close eye on him down at the garage. If it gets to be too much, we will pull back. But he seems to want to try this and let's not put a damper on so soon. Let's just play it by ear, and see how it goes."

I didn't hear what was said next, for the discussion lowered in decibels. I headed back up the stairs to my bedroom and was sitting at my desk when Dad came in to tell me the verdict.

"Pete, your mother and I have agreed to give this a try and see how it goes. If it is too much for you to handle, we will reconsider. But if you still want to do it, come on down to the garage tomorrow and I will have Leonard Callahan introduce you to the mechanics."

Leonard Callahan was the foreman, the man in charge of dealing with customers bringing in their vehicles for repair and assigning the task to one of the four mechanics. He was a big man, but gentle in his firmness. He moved easily between the "front office" as the mechanics called the showroom and offices of Wilson and Smith up front, and the "back room" as they called their space. Dad trusted Mr. Callahan, and the mechanics respected him. So I could not have been placed in better hands for my first official introduction to the men I would be working around for the next several years of my life.

"SHORTY JOHNSON"
AND THE OTHERS

Shorty" Johnson occupied stall #2 of the back room. Stall #1 was reserved for the "boss," or "J.R." I was soon to learn that was what the men of the back room called Dad. That is how I came up with the name "J.O." pinned on me. However, "Shorty" Johnson had a few other favorites of his own, when he wanted to get my immediate attention. But first, back to stall #1.

Stall #1 lay closest to the front office. When Dad wanted to play mechanic he could readily change into his work overalls and come back to align the front end of some customer's car. Dad didn't actually play at being a mechanic. All of the full-time mechanics knew that Dad was handy with the tools and that he had been away to Detroit for several weeks of special training in front end alignment. He knew this work better than any of them. And he seemed to enjoy crawling underneath the jacked up vehicle to check the frame for any damage and adjust the steering and wheel alignment, far more so than running the front office.

Mr. Callahan would always alert the mechanics that J.R. was about to enter their private space with the forewarning: "Okay, men. Clean up your act. I just assigned the boss a job."

Soon thereafter, Dad would come through the passageway dressed in his grease-stained overalls and claim stall #1.

But the real power of the back room resided in stall #2. That was the domain of "Shorty" Johnson. True to his name, he was somewhat short in stature. However, I never saw him back down to any man. He had dropped out of school at the end of the 8th grade and had spent his years from that time until now as an auto mechanic. He was what was known in the trade as a "hands-on natural" who seemed born with a sixth sense of what makes an automobile engine run well. And he was the clearly acknowledged leader of the back room mechanics. So Mr. Callahan led me straight away to stall #2 for my official introduction to Mr. Johnson.

"Shorty, I want you to meet John, Jr. who will be joining us. He is to take over from John Goggin the clean-up work," Mr. Callahan announced.

Mr. Johnson didn't say anything. His head was still buried beneath the raised hood of an old Plymouth coupe he was working on. He slowly turned his head sideways in my direction and stared at the young whippersnapper standing in his space.

"John, Jr. who?" he blurted out. "You mean J.R.'s kid?"

"That's right," Mr. Callahan answered. "J.R.'s son."

"Well, I'll be full of shit. You don't say. We're going to have the boss's kid running around our space keeping an eye on us and reporting back up front."

With that outburst, Shorty emerged from beneath the hood and took his stance directly in front of me. Slowly he looked me up and down. Then up and down again for good measure. And finally he settled his gaze on my feet.

I shuffled uncomfortably on my feet under his continued gaze downward. I was in my growing stage and my feet, then a full size ten, had far outstripped the rest of my body. My hands had also grown faster than the rest of my frame, but I assumed all my body parts would eventually catch up. In the meantime, all I could do was live with the fact that my feet and hands did seem somewhat out of proportion to the rest of my body.

"I'll be damned," he uttered. "Those are the biggest underpinnings I ever did see on a young wart hog. Kid, if you ever do grow into them feet of yours, you sure are going to be one hell've a big man."

With that he gave me a big wink, stuck out his grease covered hand, and said: "Welcome aboard, J.O. Just call me Shorty. Old Shorty will watch out for you and keep you out of trouble with the rest of them troublemakers who live back here."

From that day forward I was known in the back room as "J.O." The rest of the troublemakers were quickly introduced by Shorty, who assumed that Mr. Callahan had done his duty and had best off retreat to the front office, leaving the remaining introductions in the hands of the real boss of the back room.

"Now next to me, in stall #3, is Don. He may look vicious, but he don't mean no harm. Next to Don is Big Al. Al's the quiet one. But don't let that fool you. He knows his cars. Then at the far end is the 'professor.' He's okay, even thought he gets a little carried away in his head at times, and keeps his nose in a book a little too much."

I later learned that the professor's real name was Bill Sands, and that he was a student in mechanical engineering at the School of Mines. He had grown up in St. Louis and after graduating from high school had gone to work as an auto mechanic at a large Chrysler dealership in downtown St. Louis. After working for ten years, he decided to come to the School of Mines and get an engineering degree. To support his wife and young daughter, he was working for Wilson-Smith

Motor Company part-time and going to school full-time. Bill was hard-working. I got to know Bill pretty well over the next couple of years, until he graduated and went back to St. Louis to work for McDonald Aircraft Corporation as an engineer.

Later on, I was to meet Charlie Daniels and Dale Johnson, no relation to Shorty. They were the bodyshop men and worked in the loft above the back room. The loft was the second floor of the garage. It had its own back entrance off an alley that connected with 7th Street. That is where the bodywork was done on cars and trucks that had been smashed up in accidents.

Charlie and Dale had their own private empire up in the loft, far removed from the front office and Shorty Johnson. Since they had their own entrance they could come and go as they pleased. I quickly found the loft a place of retreat and respite and spent many an hour being taught the skills of bodyshop work, and learning the wisdom of life from Charlie and Dale. It also gave me my own private entrance and exit, so I could come and go as I pleased without having to pass through the front office.

My primary task was to keep the back room clean. But, I was quickly given other tasks as the men out back saw fit. Short Johnson was the first to expand my duties. This was done on day one on the job. After being shown exactly how he wanted his tools replaced in his chest and on his work bench, after being cleaned, and where he wanted me to stack clean rags, and hang up his cords and light, he showed me his coffee cup.

"I like my coffee strong and black and hot when I arrive in the morning," Short stated.

I assumed that this meant he expected me to greet him each

morning upon his arrival with his own cup full of coffee. I was right, as he made clear. So on day two on the job I greeted Shorty with his hot cup of coffee. After handing it to him I went back to work cleaning up on the far side near the grease rack.

A few seconds later I heard a huge loud "agh" coming from the direction of stall #2.

This was immediately followed by: "My god, I've been poisoned."

And then came the follow-up: "Hey, warthog, get them big paddle feet of yours over here on the double."

When I arrived Shorty was standing in a purple rage holding his empty coffee cup in his right hand and motioning to the floor with his left. I saw a large swath of hot coffee at his feet, either spit or thrown on the concrete floor.

"When I want coffee, I mean coffee. Hot and black. I don't want no soapy water. This stuff tasted awful. What did you give me? A cup full of water laced with soap?"

Obviously, Shorty was not overly pleased with my first attempt at making coffee. So, I was taken by the arm and shown my way up front to the coffee maker, and given a firm lesson in the fine art of brewing coffee.

My learning took a bent for the better after day two on the job. Shorty did honor his word to take me under his wing. He showed me how to take off the head of an engine. He explained the functioning of the drive shaft and the pistons, and how the spark plugs ignite the compressed air and gas mixture to drive the pistons downward and rotate the drive shaft. He taught me how to adjust the carburetor and the fuel pump to get the right mixture. He even tried to pass on his skill of listening to the hum of the engine to assess whether the tuning was good.

Bill Sands taught me how to raise the grease rack slowly and carefully once a car had been driven into place. And, once the car had been hoisted above my head, how to locate all the grease openings under the body and compress the grease gun for the right amount of lubricant.

Up in the loft Dale and Charlie taught me the skills of bodywork. I soon mastered the task of pounding out dented fenders and door panels, filling the small indentations with softened lead, and then smoothing down the lead fill with a metal rasp until no sign of a dent was left to show. I was taught how to spray the primary on the raw metal surfaces, carefully moving the spray nozzle over the surface at the right speed, and then to follow it up with the finish color coat.

John Goggin taught me how to look up a part number in the MoPar manuals and then locate the part in the appropriate bin or shelf. I didn't need any instruction in how to clean the inside of a new car or to polish the outside. All of this seemed to keep the principal owner and lead front-end alignment mechanic happy. What did not seem to please him so much was my tendency to spend a lot of my time chewing the fat with the mechanics.

I learned that Charlie, up in the loft, had landed at the beaches in Normandy and had taken a couple of machine gun bullets in his right leg. I guess that is why he walked with a slight limp. His best buddy was blown out of the water right in front of him as they were wading ashore at the beachhead. Charlie would describe, in detail to me, his thoughts as he watched his best buddy slip below the surface of the water in a pool of blood where seconds before he had been propping up Charlie's courage to keep trudging forward.

Bill Sands shared with me his dreams of becoming a professional engineer with a full-fledged college degree, and how he was the first in his family to ever attend college. He and his wife were committed to seeing this through, but it was tough being 28 years old and going back to college with a bunch of young 18 year olds fresh out of high school.

Even Shorty Johnson confided in me that he wished he had gone to high school and graduated with a degree. He encouraged me to continue my education and not drop out of high school.

Every once in awhile Dad would call me into his office for some job counseling.

"Now, Pete, I know you enjoy talking to the men out back, but don't get in their way. Watch your time."

That was the extent of his counseling. I took heed of the warning and did watch that I not become a nuisance to the men. But they seemed to enjoy sharing their dreams and thoughts with me as much as I liked listening and learning from them.

BIG RED: MEN AND THEIR MACHINES

ROLLA HAD A DIRT STOCK CAR RACING track out west of town down the road past the headquarters of Mark Twain National Forest. It was not an impressive track by stock car racing standards of the day. But it was the only track in that part of Missouri. And Shorty Johnson felt that Wilson-Smith Motor Company was not worth his time unless the company was represented at the local track with its own stock car. So that is how I was introduced to the sport of stock car racing.

Shorty and the other mechanics picked out an old used Dodge off the back lot that they wanted to turn into a full-fledged stock car. Dad reluctantly gave in, and the task of converting what had been slated for the junk pile into a sleek racing machine was begun.

After shutting down the back room at noon on Saturdays, Shorty and Big Al and Don set to work installing a powerful new engine. Charlie and Dale installed rollover bars and reinforced the side panels and streamlined the body to reduce friction. The car body was painted white with the fenders painted a bright red. Big blue stars were painted on the side doors. It was a sight to behold.

A driver needed to be recruited, but Shorty had his contacts. Jackie Campbell soon appeared on the scene to inspect the new racing machine in the making. He listened to the engine quietly roar in stall #2 and took it out for a couple of test drives with Shorty riding shotgun. Evidently, he liked what he drove, and he signed on to be the first driver of the Wilson-Smith Motor Company racing machine.

Jackie Campbell was not from Rolla. He lived down the highway at Licking. But Shorty assured us that he was well-qualified as a stock car driver, having come out of the flats of Oklahoma, where he was known as one tough aggressive driver with a will to win. Shorty wanted nothing less than victories and trophies which were to be added to the aura of stall #2.

On opening day of racing season in early June of 1953, we departed the garage for the racetrack. I went out early with Shorty and the men, to be followed later by Dad and the rest of the family. We towed the red-white-blue machine onto the track and Jackie climbed into the driver's seat. He and the other drivers then took their machines around the track for warm-up runs. Lots were drawn and we pulled the inside slot in row #2. Not a bad position. The first race was slated for 30 laps, nothing too strenuous this early in the season.

The cars all lined up at the start with engines roaring and the crowd cheering and the blood surging in anticipation of the start of the racing season. The race announcer was perched high above the back of the stands blaring out the lineup, but no one could hear over the high-pitched din.

The starting official moved forward, checkered flag in hand. He raised it slowly above his head, drawing attention to himself and the events about to unfold down at the starting line. With a grand sweep of his right arm the starting flag soared down and across his body and up again. The racers leaped forwards, down the straightaway, directly in front of the stands. They headed bunched in a tight pack into the first turn. Jackie Campbell kept his cool and maintained his position. Shorty yelled into my ear over the din that Jackie was simply taking the measure of the other drivers and their machines.

They roared through lap one, followed by lap two, then lap three, still tightly bunched. Then gaps started to appear as some drivers began to lag and others simply seemed to lack the willpower to dogfight it out for the lead. But Jackie kept the Wilson-Smith Motor Company racing machine near the front end of the pack, still keeping his cool according to Shorty.

The laps flew by as the racers circled the backside of the track and roared down the straightaway and roared off and around again. Jackie was still keeping his cool. He was in the front pack, but he was not in the lead. Lap 24 came and roared off. . .lap 25. . .lap 26. . .lap 27. Only three more laps left. Still Jackie was near the front, several cars from the lead, keeping his cool. Concern began to surface down in the Wilson-Smith Motor Company racing pit.

I was standing beside Shorty, and Big Al was on my left. Charlie and Don were checking out spare tire replacements behind us. They wanted to be ready for a fast tire change if called upon. But the unspeakable continued to swell up in all our minds. Was Jackie just going to keep his cool through the entire race and come out second or third? That was not what we came to see. The thought of the yellow car from Ford Motor Company or the black and white car from McKibbon Tires carrying the checkered flag around the victory lap was too much to contemplate.

The lead cars roared down the straightaway, three in number. Jackie was in the pack of three which gave us some glimmer of hope for victory. But McKibbon Tires held the lead, and there didn't seem to be any sign of slacking off or petering out, or unexpected engine trouble. The pit crew of Wilson-Smith Motor Company began to retreat from center stage and wait out the inevitable.

Suddenly Jackie made his move. He slammed down hard on the accelerator. The big Dodge engine roared in response. Jackie banked high on the outside curve, took aim and gunned for the inside lane coming down the straightaway. He slid past the yellow Ford car and shot past the McKibbon car directly in front of the stands and roared off for the final lap in a cloud of dust. The pit crew of Wilson-Smith Motor Company ran quickly back up front to claim center stage and cheer Jackie on to victory. No more "keeping cool."

The checkered flag swept across the line in perfect timing as Jackie claimed the first victory of the season. The crowd roared in the stands and the announcer shouted in his mike above the din: "And here comes Big Red from Wilson-Smith Motor Company down the straightaway and across the finish line number one."

Jackie slowed down just long enough to grab the victory flag and hold it out the window with his left arm while he guided Big Red with his right around the track for his victory lap. He pulled slowly into the pit, crawled out the window on the driver's side of Big Red, and gave the crowd a sweeping wave. With Shorty at his side he made his way to the victory stand to claim the trophy and winner's check, the latter quickly disappearing into his overall pocket.

We loaded up Big Red, for that is the name that the Wilson-Smith Motor Company pit crew quickly adopted for our vehicle, and the name our racing machine was to be known by for the remainder of its racing life, and headed back into town.

Big Red was proudly ensconced in stall #1. The principle owner and head front-end alignment mechanic of Wilson-Smith Motor Company was going to have to look elsewhere for space to work.

Shorty wanted Big Red nearby. The rest of the pit crew agreed. The first victory trophy was placed on Shorty's bench, and I was instructed in its future care.

Big Red continued to add aura to stall #2. One victory followed another. The first victory trophy was joined by the second and the third and then the fourth. A special trophy case was secured and carefully placed on Shorty's work bench. The photographer from the *Rolla Daily News* was prevailed upon to take a "professional" picture of Big Red that was prominently displayed in the case. Shorty managed to come across a victory flag that was draped down one side of the case.

Jackie was fast adding to his reputation, coming out of the flats of Oklahoma, that he was one tough aggressive driver with a will to win. Shorty began to swell with pride as his aura began to move well beyond stall #2 and over to stalls of McKibbon and Ford and the Chevrolet dealership just around the corner from 7th and Pine.

The Saturday afternoon preparation for the races took on a new sense of urgency and secrecy. Precisely at noon, the doors to the back room were shut and locked. No one but the pit crew and Wilson-Smith Motor Company mechanics were allowed to enter, unless given a special access permit by Shorty Johnson. Rumors in the local racing community of Rolla were rampant. How did Shorty and his cohorts manage to nurture more power out of Big Red's engine than those in the Fords and Chevys of other crews? Why did Big Red seem so solid and firm and grounded as it roared out of high banked curves and shot across the finish line, number one time after time?

Preparation reached a fever pitch as the "big one" approached. The "big one" was a massive one hundred lap race with a winner's prize of $5,000. Drivers and machines were expected from all across southern Missouri. Some were coming up north out of the Arkansas tracks. And rumor had it that even some machines might suddenly appear from the big time tracks in eastern Oklahoma.

Big Red was coddled and tweaked and tuned. Special fuel was mixed, always keeping within the racing rules of conduct. Special racing tires were purchased. Big Red was given a new coat of paint, with red replacing the white on the body, more in keeping with the name. Jackie Campbell took a room in Rolla to be closer to the scene.

The Wilson-Smith pit crew decided that Big Red needed to be hoisted on top of a flatbed truck for its journey out to the track. We simply could not take a chance of damaging our precious racing machine by driving it out in the mass of cars and pickups headed for the track, nor did we want to risk towing it with the wrecker.

Starting time for the "big one" was 7:00 pm. The stands were full by 5:30 pm. The Wilson-Smith pit crew had been on the scene since 4:00 pm. Jackie arrived at 6:45 pm. He didn't take any warm-up runs. That would be mingling with the riff-raff. He didn't seem nervous. That was beneath the dignity of a big time driver out of the flats of Oklahoma. He simply climbed into Big Red, ignited the engine, let it roar to life, and took his position in slot #1, row #1, earned by past victories.

The official starter took his position, flag held far above his head. He gave a long pause as the anticipation peaked. With a grand sweep of his arm, the "big one" was off and running. Jackie kept his cool. The Wilson-Smith Motor Company pit crew kept their calm. The outcome was a foregone conclusion. It was only a matter of time until Jackie and Shorty would claim the victory trophy, and Jackie would quickly pocket the $5,000 winner's check.

Then it happened! Lap 36. Big Red slammed into the high retaining wall on the backside of the track, and the right rear tire burst open. A strange liquid began to pour out from underneath Big Red. The yellow warning flag flashed. Big Red limped down into the pit. Then the red emergency stop flag flashed. All the racers came to a screeching halt, maintaining their positions at the moment of stopping the race.

Officials strode out to the backside of the track, bent down over the ground to inspect the strange liquid. The crowd suspected a gasoline leak out of Big Red. The officials bent low over the dirt, smelling the liquid. They carefully tasted the liquid. Then they conferred. The lead official turned around and with a sudden determination made his way over to Shorty Johnson and the rest of the Wilson-Smith Motor Company pit crew.

"WATER," the lead official screamed into the face of Shorty. "You got them tires of yours loaded with water. No wonder Big Red seems so grounded coming out of the curves."

"What do you mean water?" responded Shorty, putting on his most naïve face.

"I mean to tell you that you have been filling up your rear tires with water to get more rear-end traction. You know the rules."

Shorty sensed that the end was at hand, so he simply responded: "What's a little water among friends?"

"Don't go giving me none of your bullshit, Shorty Johnson. I know you too well. You and Big Red, and the rest of your motley crew, can just pack up and head back into town. Your racing season is done. I'll be down first thing Monday morning to collect back all them trophies you got tucked away."

With that the official turned around, and with a wave of the flag, proceeded to start the race where it had suddenly and unexpectedly left off.

Big Red sat out the rest of the race in the pit. The Wilson-Smith Motor Company pit crew sat on the ground on the backside of Big Red, out of sight of the stands and anyone else within range. The race was won by the black and white car from McKibbon. The victory lap was taken. And the Wilson-Smith Motor Company pit crew continued to sit on the ground on the backside of Big Red. Long after the stands had cleared and the other racers had departed, Big Red was loaded onto the flatbed and hauled back to 7th and Pine.

Big Red was parked in the back lot and covered with a tarp. There it sat for the next year or two, slowly rusting away. Jackie Campbell checked out of his room in Rolla late that night and was never seen again. Rumor had it he moved to North Carolina where stock car racing was really big time. And Shorty Johnson went back to being the boss of the back room and listening to the hum of engines under repair in stall #2.

MR. GOGGIN NEEDS
A FEW DAYS OFF

IT WAS A DAY IN EARLY JUNE. School had just let out for summer vacation a couple of weeks before. The air was warm and clean, and the sky a deep clear blue. The heat and humidity of a normal Ozark summer were still a ways off. It was one of those special days when I could smell the grass growing and hear the clear sparkling water splashing over the rocks down at Beaver Creek. By this time tomorrow I would be camped above Beaver Creek, my sleeping bag and .22 rifle and a good book at my side. It would be my first get-a-way time to myself of the summer season. I could hardly wait for the next day to arrive. But for right now, I was busy at work at the garage.

I arrived at my usual time of 6:15 am, and John Goggin and I opened up the garage for daily business. I had completed my clean-up of the back room, greased and changed the oil in a couple of cars, and eaten my lunch of two bologna and cheese sandwiches, a bag of potato chips and a Pepsi. By mid-afternoon, I was busy in the showroom polishing a new car.

Dad was in his office punching away at the daily billings. John Goggin had not returned from lunch. It was a quarter to three. This was not normal for him. He was always very punctual about getting back from lunch at 2:00 p.m. I didn't give it much thought, assuming that he was feeling the laziness of the early summer day, like the rest of us.

I was so absorbed in finishing my polishing job, and thinking about Beaver Creek tomorrow, I didn't notice Dad standing over me as I bent down, putting the final polishing touches on the new Dodge sedan.

"Pete, why don't you hop on your bike and peddle out to John's house to see if everything is okay," Dad said to me.

"I'm on my way," I tossed over my shoulder, as I headed to my bike.

It was a quick ride down 7th Street to where it runs into the highway, then left along the highway to the road leading off to the Goggin's white frame house. I left my bike at the bottom of the steps and bounded up the steps, two at a time, feeling strong and free. As I reached the top step, I paused to get my bearings and saw Mr. Goggin sitting on the grass underneath the clothesline to the right of the house. Fresh laundry was pinned to the lines, towels and sheets blowing gently in the breeze.

On the ground beside Mr. Goggin, lay his wife Ellie. She seemed very still and quiet. Mr. Goggin was sitting right next to her holding her hand in his right hand and stroking her head with his left.

"Ellie. . .my dear Ellie. . .Ellie.. .dear Ellie. . ," he was slowly and softly repeating again and again, as his hand gently caressed her forehead.

I just stood stock still watching and absorbing the scene being played out across the lawn. I sensed immediately that Mrs. Goggin lay dead on the grass, and that Mr. Goggin had found her there when he arrived for lunch. She had obviously been out pinning up the laundry when she collapsed to the ground. A half-empty laundry basket lay near her side.

A large lump swelled up in my chest and warm tears slowly began to form in the corners of my eyes. I wasn't feeling morbid. And I wasn't panicked. I was simply filling up from way down deep with the picture of the two of them sitting together on the grass. Fifty-eight years of marriage. John had been 20 and Ellie 18. Fifty-eight years of living together. Now they were spending their last few moments together before Mr. Goggin called the coroner's office.

I slowly turned around and walked carefully down, picking out the steps, one at a time. The ride back to 7th and Pine was even slower. I parked my bike out front of the garage and walked into the showroom. Dad was standing there, waiting my return.

"What did you find Pete?" Dad quietly asked.

I stood still, my eyes focused on the concrete floor of the showroom. I waited a long time before answering. Dad stood patiently by.

"Mr. Goggin is okay," I answered. "He just needs a few days off to himself."

I didn't say more. I didn't need to. Dad sensed what had happened. He came over slowly, put his arm around my shoulder, and simply said.

"Pete, you've had a long day of it. Why not call it quits and head home?"

john oliver wilson

WINDOW TO THE OUTSIDE WORLD

john oliver wilson

SCOTT'S DRUGSTORE

SCOTT'S DRUGSTORE SITS AT THE CORNER of Eighth and Pine, center stage of the Rolla of my day. The store occupied the bottom floor of a two story, red brick structure that had been built sometime around 1880 or 1890. It was a classic small town structure, fronting on the main street of town, located on the corner so that it commanded presence on two sides, a step above the storefront structures that "lesser" enterprises occupied.

The drugstore was named for founder and initial owner, John W. Scott, who arrived in Rolla in 1886 to attend the School of Mines. But he was not destined to become an engineer. It was music that was his passion, and he became what local historians called "Rolla's Man of Music." When he arrived Rolla was apparently lacking a cultural base, at least when it came to music or at least music as understood by Mr. Scott. He quickly organized a band at the School of Mines, a local town band, a symphony orchestra and a town chorus of some fifty voices.

All of these musicians needed instruments and sheet music. That is where Scott's Drugs came into being, in 1909, to be exact. Scott's Drugs did stock the usual selection of ointments and salves and corn plasters for sore toes that one would expect to find in a drugstore at the turn of the century. But it also stocked a lot more—brass cornets and trumpets, trombones and clarinets, snare drums and base drums for his bands, and violins and violas, cellos and base fiddles for his orchestra, along with sheet music for his chorus. All were arrayed in large glass cases lining the walls of his new drugstore.

But Scott's Drugs was far more than just ointments for what ails you, and musical instruments for what inspires you. At the far back of the store was a bookstore for the students up at the School of Mines. Finally, there was the fountain itself. No self-respecting small town drugstore at the turn of the century could function without a soda fountain to distill ice cream and milkshakes and root beer floats. The standard swivel stools were arrayed on one side of the counter facing a large mirror so that no one could enter the drugstore, without being recognized by those sitting at the counter. Pasted to the face of the mirror was a list of "flavors of the day" and prices for everything from a simple soda to a banana split with all the trimmin's.

Not much had changed in Scott's Drugstore from the days of John W. Scott and 1909 until I arrived some fifty years later. Scott's Drugstore still commanded center stage at Eighth and Pine. It still had a soda fountain up front, long cases of music instruments along the walls, and shelves stocked with Preparation H, and cold tablets, and bottles of aspirin of every shape and variety. The bookstore stocked texts for a new generation of Miners. Only Mr. Scott was missing. But his grandson, John R. Morris, was now the owner and manager.

Johnnie Morris, as he was known to the locals, adults and kids alike, was a "worldly man" by Rolla standards. Some of the locals talked, of course well behind his back, that he had gone to the big city of Chicago, and got educated, and then served in the U.S. Navy during the tail end of World War II, and got worldly. Coming back to Rolla, he had "modernized" the Scott's Drugstore of his grandfather into something that belonged in the expanding suburbs of St. Louis rather than at Eighth and Pine in Rolla.

Be that as it may, those of us who had never been to Chicago, or college away from Rolla, thought that Johnnie Morris and his modernized Scott's Drugstore was the end all of all end alls. It was here that we climbed up on the swivel stools, as soon as our growing legs and horded allowances and the freedom to roam up and down Pine Street on our own, allowed. It was here that we could meet our friends and keep an eye on the coming and goings of the locals and the tourists who drove into town from Route 66, to take in the sights of the "gateway to the Ozarks." It was here that we began to mingle with the Miners, and work out our version of the "town-gown" conflict that all small towns with colleges learn to work out. And, it was here that Johnnie Morris employed a few of the select youth of Rolla with the intent of expanding their horizons beyond the bounds of Rolla and Pine Street.

I never knew how Johnnie Morris selected those he targeted for "broadening." All I know is that one warm, bright summer morning in mid-May, Dad called me into his office at Wilson-Smith Motor Company. I had just finished greasing a Plymouth jacked up on the rack in back and was getting ready to clean up my grease stained hands and arms, and head home for a day down on the Gasconade River in my canoe.

"Pete, Johnnie Morris would like to talk to you. He's up at Scott's right now in his office. Called to see if you were around. Told him I would pass on the message."

"What's he want to see me for?" I queried Dad.

"Don't know. Why don't you go up and find out?" was all I was able to get out of Dad.

I suspected that Dad knew full well what was up. But, clearly he wasn't about to give me a heads-up. This was going to be between Mr. Morris and myself. At this stage of my life I still referred to Johnnie Morris as Mr. Morris, for I had yet to earn the right of local familiarity. That would come later.

I cleaned up, trying to remove the smell of grease, scrubbing hard with a cleaning paste that has a unique smell of its own. There was no way I was going to get rid of the tell-tale signs that I was entering the bright gleaming confines of Scott's Drugs, smelling like a grease monkey. What would Mr. Morris think on our first official "business" encounter? I had no choice but to go forth, smelling as I did.

"Mr. Morris, I understand you want to see me," I announced upon knocking on the open doorway to his office, tucked behind the pharmacy at the back end of Scott's.

"Come in. . .come in," Mr. Morris invited with a friendly smile, quickly putting me at ease with his inviting manner. "Sit down and let's chat a bit."

"I know you have been working for your Dad for the past several years down at the garage," Mr. Morris quickly stated once I took a seat on a folding metal chair alongside his desk. "And I know that things are going well for you up at high school. You just finished your freshman year and are about to begin this fall as a sophomore. Still got a few years to think about college and beyond. No need to rush. Still a lot to learn about life."

This seemed to me a strange opening to our chat a bit. I kept quiet wondering where all of this was headed. Not that I had to wait long. Mr. Morris was not one to waste words or time.

"Ever thought about coming up to Scott's Drug and working for me? I need some more help behind the fountain and have kept my eye on you for some time now as a likely man for the job. Also, need some help in the bookstore once the Miners come back this fall for the next term. Know you are quite a student and working around the textbooks might be of some interest."

I felt my head begin to swim and my stomach go a little tight. It had never entered my mind that one day I might work at Scott's. I always assumed that I would finish out my work days before heading off to college down at the garage. To move from Seventh and Pine where Wilson-Smith Motor Company was located up to Eighth and Pine and Scott's Drugs was far more than just a short shift in location.

It was moving to a completely different world. It was a world of glamour and visibility and commerce. It was a world where students and locals gathered to vent on the issues of the day, and where tourists dropped in to take in the sights and smells of a small town before heading west to bigger sights and more lasting smells. It was a world with windows far beyond the large plate glass ones that gave an unobstructed view of the comings and goings on Pine Street.

"Yes sir, I have thought about it quite a bit. But I never thought I would have the opportunity. It would be quite an honor to work at Scott's." I responded.

This was stretching the truth a little, for while I was on firm ground in stating that I would be honored to work at Scott's, I was on far less firm ground in stating that I had thought about it a lot. I had never assumed I would have the opportunity. Now it was staring me right in the face, and I had jumped at the offer. And, rather than feeling elated and exuberant, my stomach gave a wrench and pangs of doubt rushed into my still swimming head. Did I really what to leave the garage and Shorty Johnson and all the other men who had nurtured me along the way? Would I miss being around Dad every day? Would I measure up to Mr. Morris' expectations? Did I really want to grow up this fast?

Mr. Morris sat quietly for a few moments while all of this sank in, but he must have been reading my mind, or at least sensing that this was not such a cut and dried decision as I had blurted out in my initial response. He then broke the silence in a calm and secure voice.

"Your Dad and I have talked this through, and he thinks it is time for you to move on. Not that he won't miss you down at the garage, but working at Scott's will give you a broader view on life. And, it is not as if you are moving to some foreign country. We are friendly people up here at Eighth and Pine," he said with a broad smile. "Think it over and let me know in a day or two what you would like to do. I'll be here."

I thanked Mr. Morris and promised that I would get back to him soon, and that I was really honored at the thought of working at Scott's. I didn't want him to get the idea that I was hesitant or unappreciative, for I wasn't. It was just that life had taken a sudden and abrupt change since I left home early this morning for the garage. I needed some time to think this through. I needed to get my canoe down on the Gasconade post-haste.

So it was that I came under the wing of Johnnie Morris and joined the cadre of select Rolla youth who were chosen to have their "horizons broadened." For the next three years of my life in Rolla, I was to witness a lot of characters pass through Scott's Drug and those big glass windows that opened onto Pine Street and beyond.

I'VE FOUND ME A HILLBILLY!

IT WAS A WARM AFTERNOON IN EARLY July, and I was busy scooping ice cream and pumping sodas when I noticed a middle-aged couple trailing a teenaged daughter and a tall, lanky boy of around twelve or thirteen come through the big glass front doors of Scott's. They quickly looked around, found an empty booth right across from the soda fountain counter and sat down, awaiting service. They were not locals, all of whom I knew. Besides, locals of the adult variety did not haul their teenaged kids into Scott's when they wanted to get a soda. And their teenaged off-spring were not about to be seen in Scott's accompanied by parents. Obviously, they were tourists.

The teenaged daughter sported a blond ponytail down the back of her sundress, and she showed plenty of development up front. Things like this did not go unnoticed by the soda fountain jerks behind the counter. We quickly took her measure and hauled out the half-dollar we kept by the cash register for just such occasions. I won the flip to see who would get the honor of serving her, along with her "old man," busy wiping the sweat from his balding forehead, and her mother, fidgeting with her pocketbook in search of some long lost comb or lip stick or who knows what. I tried to ignore the kid brother who looked like he might be trouble a-brewing.

"Traveling through?" I asked, handing them our one-page menu of offerings.

"Yeah," was all I got from the old man. "Traveling through." The ponytail seemed oblivious to my sudden presence, looking through me as if I were little more than a local yokel, not worth a pleasant smile or even a nod of recognition.

"Where you all from?" I tried again.

"Chicago," was all I got in return from the old man and the ponytail staring off into space. Obviously, they had driven down Route 66 and had been lured into Rolla by large signs just east of town announcing "Rolla: Gateway to the Ozarks." Many a tourist had stumbled their way into Scott's Drugs by way of these signs.

Forget the ponytail, I thought to myself. Get their order and hope for better with the next booth of tourists. I quickly served them the ice cream concoctions they ordered, along with four large Cokes. As they ate and drank they seemed to become more relaxed, and the ponytail even flashed me a smile as I moved behind the counter serving other customers perched on the stools. Maybe they were just hot and tired from their long trip down 66, I thought to myself, and weren't such bad folk after all. They seemed to be settling into their booth as they looked around the drugstore at the locals perched along the counter and the music instruments lining the cabinets down the side wall. Then the old man motioned to me with his hand.

"Son," he said, when I moved to the booth to be of service. "You from around here?"

"Yeah, born and raised in Rolla," I answered.

"Is this really the Gateway to the Ozarks," he then queried.

I explained that Rolla was situated on the northern edge of a very large geologic formation of limestone and dolomite laid down by an ancient sea a billion or more years ago. That it had been uplifted by forces not fully understood. And that millions of years of erosion had worn the mountains down from their high peaks into the rolling hills.

"I don't mean the geology of the Ozarks," abruptly interrupted the ponytail's old man. "I mean the real Ozarks, moonshiners, mules, hillbillies. That's what we came to see."

Now I knew a lot more about geology than I did about moonshiners or mules or hillbillies. But I was not about to admit ignorance on such important matters, especially with the ponytail sitting there with what appeared to me to be a newfound interest in the locals, one in particular.

"Well then, you all are going to be around awhile."

"Depends on what we find of interest. My hobby is photography, and I like to take pictures of the local lore when I travel," the old man responded. "Where would you recommend I drive to find a moonshiner working his still or a mule or a hillbilly plowing a field? Those would be great shots to take back home."

I had only stumbled across what might be called a moonshiner a couple of times, on my hiking up and down the Ozark hills south of town. And then I beat a quick retreat, for those who still make their own corn whiskey from mash are not prone to welcome outsiders. They generally have a passel of coon dogs around their spreads, and those dogs can tree intruders of two legs, as well as four. So I was of little help in suggesting a willing moonshiner who might pose for tourists from Chicago.

Mules were a little easier to come up with. Missouri mules are a stubborn lot, as are Missourian's in general, hence our unofficial State motto: Stubborn as a Missouri Mule. The scrub farms sprinkled through the hills around Rolla still sported a few mules. You could find them simply by driving south on Route 63 to any marked county road, which would lead you back into the hollows and along the creek beds. But, I sensed my Chicago tourist customers would not be interested in venturing too far off Route 66, on their way west. To plunge down Route 63, into the heart of the Ozarks, would be going too far.

I didn't know how to address the issue of hillbillies. I had never met a hillbilly, but was well aware that this was not a moniker that was viewed with great esteem by locals, myself included. Webster's defines a hillbilly as "a person who lives in or comes from the mountains or backwoods, especially of the South: a somewhat contemptuous term." Those of us born and raised in Rolla did not view ourselves as coming from the backwoods.

I shrugged my shoulders and said that I couldn't be of much help in their quest for a moonshiner or a mule or a hillbilly. We did have a local Chamber of Commerce office down the street, and it was probably open. They might be of some help. So much for flirting with the "ponytail" from Chicago. I had better things to do, and returned to the back of the soda fountain trying to look busy washing a stack of dirty ice cream dishes.

A few minutes later I glanced over to the booth, expecting my tourist customers from Chicago to be getting up to pay their tab and heading out the door to the Pennant Hotel or the Quality Court, never to be seen again in Scott's Drugs. But no. The ponytail's "old man" was signaling me to return quickly to the booth, with the rapid motion of his hand. So I walked to the booth as nonchalantly as I could.

"Look. . .look," he blurted out. "There's a real live hillbilly standing over there in the back of the store. Why didn't you tell me? Do you think he would mind if I took his picture?"

I looked towards the back of the store where the old man was motioning and saw a tall middle aged man standing talking to Don, the pharmacist. He was garbed in bib overalls that were somewhat soiled with red clay dirt and was wearing a well worn blue denim shirt, topped off with a straw hat that was the worst for the wear. All he lacked was a corn cob pipe to pass for what one might think of as a real live hillbilly.

"Well, you might be right," I responded, suddenly sensing that this could be getting interesting. "But I wouldn't recommend shoving a camera smack in front of his face and asking him to pose. Hillbillies can be a little cantankerous at times. He might just fetch his shotgun from the back of his pickup, and let you have a load of buckshot you-know-where." And with that, I patted my backside to emphasize the you-know-where.

"You don't say," he exclaimed. "Then I better be a little careful. What if I just scooted myself down the aisle, out of sight, towards the end of the booths and snapped his picture from over that counter back there. He would never see me."

"Be my guest," I replied.

By now, the entire counter of locals was riveted on the actions unfolding at the booth as we watched. The man carefully scooted himself to the aisle, crouched down, as if stalking an Indian in the wilderness, and worked his way carefully down the aisle towards the back counter, keeping a wary eye on his hillbilly. He moved his camera into place. We heard a distinct. . .click one. . .click two. . .click three. Three pictures, soon to be on their way to the backyard barbeque of his Chicago home.

He quickly returned to the booth, a big smile across his face, obviously ready to move on. He slapped down a $5 bill, to pay for a $4 tab, leaving me a $1 tip, unheard of in those days. Locals did not tip other locals who happened to be serving them at Scott's Drugs. He motioned to his tribe to follow him out the door.

I looked across the store at his "hillbilly," who seemed oblivious to what had just happened. He and Don, the pharmacist, were still in deep conversation. Then, I looked out the large plate glass windows and saw the "ponytail" in the back seat of a large white Cadillac sedan, with Illinois license plates, slowly pull out and head up Pine Street towards Route 66.

I never did find out where they were going. Maybe Oklahoma to capture on Kodak a picture of a real live Indian, one of those who work at the numerous tourist traps sprinkled along Route 66 selling Indian souvenirs made in China. Or, they might be headed into Texas to capture a "bow-legged cowboy" striding down the main street of some small Texas town.

I just didn't have the heart to tell them, before they bolted out the door of Scott's Drugstore, that their real live hillbilly was none other than Dr. Harold Q. Fuller, Chairman of the Physics Department at the School of Mines.

It just so happened that Dr. Fuller raised prize hogs out on a small farm at the edge of town, as a means to relax. When he wasn't busy lecturing on quantum physics he could be found slopping feed to his hogs. Undoubtedly, he had just come by Scott's while in town picking up some feed for his hogs. But I didn't think that it was any of our tourist's business. They got what they wanted—their real live hillbilly, even though he sported a PhD in physics to complement his bib overalls.

GONNA STRIKE IT RICH

MINERS ARE BACK IN TOWN . . .Scott's Drugs . . .forget it . . .those Miners take over the counter and the booths, and shove us aside. That was the view of the Rolla High School males when summer came to a close and the fall was marked by the beginning of the new academic year at the School of Mines. The Rolla High School females had a different take on the matter. Many of them dated the Miners, much to the consternation of the Rolla High School males.

As I entered Scott's, to begin the new academic year, I expected the usual crowd of Miners sitting at the counter or the booths. I had gotten to know many. They would come down from their dorm rooms to Scott's to slowly work their way through a soda or sundae, while they did their homework.

Scott's was a favorite alternative to a hot and crowded dorm room shared with a couple of others, or the stuffy library. It was a hangout, not for idle chatter, but for serious homework. And so I got to know Gene and Jeff, and a host of others, as they worked their way through problem sets in physics, chemistry and calculus. They even gave me a set of problems, and guided me through the same exercises they were doing. Not that I could match them in their skills, but they quickly introduced me to physics, chemistry and calculus as well.

When I walked through the big glass doors fronting Pine Street that early fall day, I fully expected to see the usual gang of Miners sitting up and down the counter and spilling over into the booths, busy discussing the beginning of the new academic year. I was looking forward to continuing my "problem set" learning sessions.

They would usually look my way when I walked through the door, and greet me with something like, "Hey, John, you still around? The boredom of the summer didn't get to you without us around to harass you. Any new good-looking girls come to town while we were gone?"

But that particular day there was no such friendly banter of warm greeting. Not even a glance in my direction. They were all huddled down at the far end of the soda counter, a dozen or more, engrossed in something placed on the counter.

"Move it down the counter another 24 inches," came the order from some Miner buried deep in the huddle. Then I heard a distinct click...click...click. "Another 24 inches."

Again a distinct click.....click.....click, only this time a little slower. "Now let's test it down the aisle so we can get more distance. Jeff, you record the distances and the time between the clicks so we can study them," came the new order deep down in the huddle. And with that they placed what looked like a rock on the floor, about three feet down the aisle, took a metal box off the counter with a strap and a headset of earphones attached.

This process continued until they had reached the far back of the store, some 50 feet from the counter. They then all quickly gathered back around the counter with the rock and box in hand and placed both on the counter. It was then that I was noticed.

"Hey, John, welcome back. Great to see you. Get into that little white coat of yours and get to work."

"What in the world are you guys up to," I asked.

"Ever heard of a Geiger counter," one responded.

"Yeah, of course I know what a Geiger counter is," I answered.

I had never seen a real Geiger counter, but had certainly read enough about them, in *Popular Mechanics*. It was the height of the uranium rush, the mid-1950's. Newspapers and magazines were full of stories about geologists scouring the plains of Colorado, New Mexico, and Nevada in search of uranium ore. Miners were being lured to the western plains by mining companies, who employed them during the summer break, outfitted them with a jeep, grub stake, and sent them off as modern day prospectors.

Not much distinguished them from the gold prospectors of the past, other than a jeep replacing a mule. They would operate on their own for days at a time, under the vast skies of the west. Clutching their Geiger counter, they would carefully map any signs of uranium ore so the mining companies could stake their claim before another Geiger counter clutching mining or geology student from another mining company beat them to the punch.

It was the stuff to get the blood stirring of any young outdoors-oriented kid of the time, especially my blood. So I was well aware of what was going on at the counter, once I learned that the metal box was a Geiger counter. I joined the huddle of miners wanting to see the Geiger counter for myself. But I wondered why the sudden interest in Geiger counters when the school year was just beginning and the mining companies wouldn't begin hiring their student prospectors until sometime in the spring.

"Why all the rush?" I asked Andy. "It's a long time before next summer."

"Didn't you hear about Charlie? It's all over campus," he answered.

Charlie had been a regular at the counter last year and was a favorite of mine. He had patiently introduced me to calculus. Charlie was a geology student and I knew he had signed on to work last summer as a uranium prospector. Anaconda Copper Company, as I recall.

"No, what about Charlie? Is he back this year to finish up?"

"Don't know. No one has seen him yet. But no need for him to come back unless he wants his degree. He hit it rich last summer."

"Rich!"

"Yeah, real rich."

"Uranium."

"No, galena."

"Galena. Common old lead!"

"Don't knock lead. It has made a lot of guys from Missouri very rich."

True. The largest lead deposits in the world are in Missouri, down near Joplin in the southwest part of the state.

Andy then told me the story, at least the version of the story that apparently was sweeping its way through the dorm halls up on campus. Charlie had been assigned to explore up and down the basins and ranges of Nevada. He was running short on his luck in finding uranium leads, but he did stumble upon an oldtime gold prospector in a bar somewhere back in the hills. The prospector had some samples of galena that he had located, but he was only interested in gold.

Charlie convinced the prospector to show him the location of the galena find. Then Charlie suggested that they stake out a claim together, but the old prospector would have none of it. He sold out his share to Charlie for a couple hundred dollars, and headed back into the hills in search of gold. Charlie staked out a claim, contacted a lead mining company, and sold out his find for a quarter million dollars!

That did it. No longer would I waste time on physics and chemistry and calculus. It was geology that I had to master, particularly field geology, how to find and identify ores that would make me rich. I quickly added a textbook on mineralogy and another on methods in field geology to my learning curve, and went to work. But it didn't take me long to discover that geology is based on a lot of physics and chemistry, and so I had to keep at those topics as well.

I then began to plot how I was going to get to the west. No way a mining company was going to grubstake a high school kid. They only hired college students who were majoring in mining or geology. But the USGS, that is the United States Geological Survey, maintained their western headquarters in Rolla, sending into the field teams of surveyors to map the Western states and then produce topographic maps in their Rolla offices.

I was sure the USGS was my ticket to the west. I got a job application and applied for a summer job as rod man on one of their surveyor teams—the person who ran ahead of the surveyors and held the rod which they sighted with their scope. It was not nearly as glamorous as having my own jeep with sleeping bag and grub in the back and whipping up and down Nevada ranges, but it would have to do. At least I would be in the west and exploring land where I would strike it rich.

By spring, I had done my homework. I knew a lot about field geology, had mastered rock and mineral identification, studied maps of Colorado and Nevada and New Mexico, areas where I knew the USGS was going to focus their survey teams that summer, and had begun to lay out my camping gear. All I needed was to get my employment contract, and I would be on my way as soon as school let out for the summer.

Finally, the letter came. I grabbed it off the pile on the front desk, ran upstairs to my bedroom, sat down at my desk and ripped it open.

"Dear Mr. Wilson. . .We are sorry to inform you . . ."

I was crushed! I sat at my desk in disbelief. No job. No summer spent exploring the west. They were only going to hire college students this year. Back to Scott's for another summer of scooping ice cream and pumping out Cokes.

AIN'T HAD NO REAL CHRISTMAS

WHILE JOHNNIE MORRIS OWNED Scott's Drug Store, it was Harold who really ran the show for those of us behind the counter. Harold was "officially" the janitor, but along the way he had gradually assumed duties as head of maintenance, storage, packing, security, and anything else that needed doing. I came under his wing to be introduced to the ways of Scott's Drug as the newest hire. Harold was an institution.

No one ever knew where Harold came from. He just appeared one day. He was a Negro as we said in those days. But no one seemed to notice he was a Negro. Race was not a big issue in Rolla.

Harold sort of kept to himself when he worked at Scott's. He "kept his cards close to his chest" as the local saying went. He never disclosed much about himself. One night, as I was cleaning down the black marble countertop at the soda fountain, and he was beginning his janitorial sweep, I asked, "Harold, you got any family?"

"You's all the family old Harold got," he answered, never breaking stride, looking straight ahead, as he pushed his broom down the aisle across from the counter where I was. I knew never to probe any more into his personal affairs, no matter how long we worked side by side.

For the next three years of my life at Scott's Drug Store, Harold and I spent a lot of time together. Or, I should say, we spent a lot of time in the same space together. We stocked shelves and moved boxes of textbooks into the back storage room. We washed down the booths and counter of the soda fountain area. We kept an eye on the comings and goings on Pine Street. We locked up the front doors at night. And yet, I never got any closer to knowing any more about Harold than when I had first asked him about his family. Maybe we were the only family he had.

I knew that Harold had a small room right above the drug store. Access to the second floor was from a steep stairway off Pine Street. Each night after locking the big glass doors of Scott's Drugs on the first floor, Harold would slowly climb the steep stairway to his "home" on the second floor.

I wondered what life was like for Harold on the second floor. Did he sit up there staring out the windows facing Pine Street, observing the comings and goings from above? Did he sit there recalling family and friends from his past? Or did he just sit there staring out into space thinking about nothing? It seemed a lonesome and sad life to me. I was surrounded by family and friends and activity. And, especially on holidays, it seemed doubly lonesome and sad. What did Harold do for Christmas?

Christmas was a very festive season for Scott's. Harold strung silver tinsel ropes from the ceiling, strung lights above the mirror behind the soda fountain counter, placed cardboard Santa Clauses on the tops of the display cases, and even decorated a Christmas tree for the front of the store. We stocked special displays of Christmas gifts and hung big red bows on the music cases that held bright shiny cornets and trumpets and trombones. We would plug in a record player and play bright, cheerful Christmas songs as we cleaned up and closed down for the night. The excitement and anticipation mounted each day as Christmas approached.

Every Christmas Eve, when we closed early at 5:00 p.m., Harold stood by the big glass front doors facing Pine Street and wished each of us a Merry Christmas as he let us out the door. Where did he go once he had seen us off? Back into the store to push his broom up and down the quiet and vacant aisles by himself, and then climb up the steep stairs to the second floor to sit and recall Christmas past?

It was the Christmas season of 1955. I was in my senior year at high school.

I was working late one night, doing my usual clean up of the soda fountain. Harold was across the store pushing his broom down the aisle. The drug store was all dressed up for Christmas. But it was quiet that night. Neither Harold nor I were in the mood for Christmas music on our plugged-in phonograph. Each of us was lost in our own thoughts, I about leaving for Michigan for Christmas with my cousins. Harold thinking about, who knows what. I watched his hunched back behind the broom and noticed that he was moving more slowly than usual down the aisle. I even imagined a tear rolling down his cheek. I wanted to walk quietly up beside him and put my arm around his shoulder and gently say: "Everything's going to be all right, Harold." But I didn't.

I stood watching him, seemingly frozen in my own reveries. Then the idea suddenly came to me. Why not make a Christmas for Harold? Why not get a Christmas tree, buy him a present, decorate his second floor home? I really got excited the more I thought about it. I began planning how I could carry out my Christmas for Harold without his suspecting anything. I only had a few days left. Not much time.

The following few days, I found a small four foot cedar in the woods of a local farmer where we cut our own Christmas tree each year. I put together a couple of strings of colored lights from those that we would not be using, along with a dozen or so colored glass balls to hang on the branches. I bought a grey wool cardigan sweater at O'Mears Mens Store, across the street. And last I pirated the key to Harold's second floor home from the office.

It was my last night working at Scott's before leaving for Michigan. The customers had all gone. I stayed to clean up the counter. Harold was in the storeroom collecting his broom. All the boxes of Christmas decorations, the gift, and the small Christmas tree were locked up in the trunk of my car. I had carefully parked down Pine Street, away from the big front windows of Scott's. I didn't want to take a chance on Harold suddenly looking out and seeing me.

Once I saw that Harold was in the storeroom, I beat a hasty path out the big glass doors, collected Christmas from the trunk, mounted the steep stairway to the second floor two steps at a time, and quickly unlocked the door to Harold's home. It was about how I had envisioned. Plain and sparse, an overstuffed chair facing out to Pine Street, a small wooden table over in the corner, a hot burner for cooking his meals and a couple of old pots sitting on top of a wooden sink counter.

I moved fast. First, the Christmas tree set in the far corner opposite the overstuffed chair so Harold could sit and enjoy the brightly lit tree. Then the two strings of lights strung and plugged in. A paper tablecloth imprinted with red poinsettias and green foliage spread over the small wooden table. A pot of red poinsettias placed in the center of the table. And finally, the brightly wrapped gift set under the Christmas tree with a tag inscribed: "To Harold. From Santa Claus." I locked the door, ran down the stairs, and headed to the store room to tell Harold good by.

Two weeks later Christmas had come and gone. I walked through the big glass doors, struck by the lack of any Christmas decorations. They had all been removed and carefully stored away for next year. No special cases of Christmas gifts on display. No red bows dressing up the shiny brass cornets and trumpets and trombones. No phonograph for playing bright and cheery Christmas tunes.

Harold saw me coming through the doors. He quickly disappeared into the storeroom. When he came out, he walked up to me holding a carefully wrapped box, all sealed up with tape.

"John, here are your lights and decorations. I wrapped them up carefully so nothing will break until next year when you need them for your tree."

He paused, looked down at his feet, glanced back up at me, and then looked me square in the face.

"That was really something you did for me. Been a long time since old Harold had a real Christmas."

This time I didn't have to imagine a tear rolling down his cheek. It was real. Harold quickly turned around, wiped his hand across his face, reached for his broom, and started down the aisle. I stood watching as he disappeared towards the back of the store, hunched over his broom. I wondered what Harold had thought about on Christmas morning as he sat in his overstuffed chair, and looked at his brightly lit Christmas tree shining out onto vacant Pine Street.

MOVIN' ON

john oliver wilson

OFF AND RUNNING!

THE UNITED STATES NAVY HAD IT DOWN. They knew how to recruit. Especially in small land-locked Midwestern towns. They simply put up great big posters showing a young Navy officer standing on the deck of a cruiser, sailing across the azure blue sea, with some Mediterranean port in the background. This was particularly effective living in Rolla, where Fort Leonard Wood was just down the road. Not that we had anything against the U.S. Army, but the comparison between standing on the deck of a Navy man-of-war in the Mediterranean sea and crawling through the dust and dirt of hot and humid Fort Leonard Wood was not even close.

About the time I was beginning to think about college, the U.S. Navy had placed one of those posters right smack in front of the Post Office on Pine Street, two blocks up from Scott's. Every day, on my way to the Post Office, I would pass by that poster. The young Navy officer was suited up in dress whites, a bright shiny sword was hanging down from his side, and his arms were crossed behind his back. He was standing with his legs astride, shoulders square, head erect and strong chin thrust forward. It said leadership and command, strange and exotic foreign ports, "Join the Navy and See the World."

I don't know exactly when the idea came to me. I think it just began as I walked day after day by that poster. All I know is that one day my future suddenly seemed clear. Go to the U.S. Naval Academy and become a Navy officer. Annapolis, that is where my future lay! But one major problem—how to get to Annapolis? I couldn't simply write for a college application, fill it out, take the required SAT tests, and write a brief statement on the reasons I wanted to go to Annapolis. I had to get a political appointment.

Unfortunately, Rolla was lacking in political appointments, or rather those who could produce such appointments. We had no U.S. Senator living in Rolla. We didn't even have a U.S. Congressman. All of those big important politicians lived in St. Louis and its surrounding suburbs, or Kansas City, or elsewhere. But none in Rolla. All we had was Judge Emery Allison who had once made a run in the primary for the U.S. Senate, on the Democratic ticket, and lost badly. He had served in the Missouri State Legislature and presumably served as the judge of some court for he carried the honorable title of Judge. Now he was practicing law in Rolla, writing out wills and negotiating business contracts, settling farm foreclosures, and passing out free advice to keep peace and order in the community.

When I was in the eighth grade, I interviewed Judge Allison. It was an article for the Rolla Junior High Gazette, our home grown school newspaper. We featured prominent Rolla citizens. So, I had a more than passing acquaintance with the honorable judge. I figured that Judge Allison was my best hope for an appointment as a Midshipmen to the U.S. Naval Academy.

On a cold day in early January of my senior year, I climbed the steep wooden steps to his second floor office. I knocked on his door.

"Come on in, the door's always open to those seeking legal counsel or just stopping by for a friendly visit," the Judge announced from inside.

I turned the knob to his door and walked in. In one corner stood a large black cast iron stove, a warm blazing fire providing heat for a cold January day. The fire smelled of oak. I loved the smell and look of an old oak burning, cast iron stove. We had once heated our kitchen with a similar stove.

Along the walls were glass fronted oak book cases all full of Missouri State Legal statutes, legal books, and other books of similar impressive bindings. The floor was bare, with the exception of a small, round, rag woven rug in the middle that gave a little sense of hominess to Judge Allison's legal office. This small town legal office seemed quaint and somewhat dated even in my day.

Diplomas from the University of Missouri were posted on the wall. There were also pictures of himself with President Harry Truman, with Senator Harry Truman, and with just plain citizen Harry Truman of Independence, the latter showed the former president in front of his home with his cane as he prepared to take his daily walk.

Judge Allison was sitting at his large, rolltop oaken desk. Its small compartments were crammed full of papers. There were stacks of legal books, more papers and the *Rolla Daily News* surrounding him.

"Well, son, good to see you. Been some time since you last paid me a visit. Have a seat." Judge Allison motioned to a wooden highback chair alongside his desk. I quickly removed my parka and gloves and woolen cap and sat down.

"What's on your mind?"

"I want to go to the Naval Academy at Annapolis. I need some help getting a political appointment. I know that you are well connected with the senators and congressmen from Missouri. Maybe you can help me get an appointment," I blurted out.

Judge Allison slowly leaned back in his swivel chair, folded his hands in front of his face with his chin resting on the top of his hands and seemed to go into deep contemplation. He sat looking at me for some time as if taking my measure. He unfolded his hands, grasped the arms of his chair with each hand, and leaned forward towards me. His face was serious, yet kind. I could sense that this was going to be a serious discussion.

"Son, I admire you for wanting to go to Annapolis. But, what do your folks think of this?"

I explained that I had not discussed this with my folks, or anyone else for that matter. It was my idea. I was in the exploring stage. I wanted to know the possibilities of getting an appointment.

The Judge slowly told me how difficult it was to get an appointment to Annapolis, and how even more difficult it was to graduate from Annapolis. The life of a Midshipman was not easy. Plebe summer. Strict discipline. Tough academic curriculum. Summer cruises. Continual harassment by upper classmen. Then the Judge explained that there was a large number of well qualified young men who lived in the home districts of Missouri senators and congressmen who got the coveted appointments.

"Son, I really think you should consider other options for college. I would really like to be of some help, and wish that I could appoint you myself. For a boy from Rolla, even with your achievements, to get an appointment to Annapolis is stretching a bit too far. Not that you wouldn't make a great Naval officer in my judgment, but we just don't have the political clout down here in the Ozarks that they do in St. Louis or Kansas City. I know that you will do well wherever you go to college. I wish you well."

With that, I rose from my chair, extended my hand, thanked him for his time, grabbed my parka and headed out the door. I felt tears begin to swell up in my eyes. I walked down the steep wooden stairs and began to go the long way towards home. I needed time to absorb what I had just been through.

All of my dreams of going to Annapolis and becoming a Naval officer seemed shattered. For the next week I just went through the motions, going to class at Rolla High School, and then off to work at Scott's Drugs in the evenings. I was in a daze. Mr. Morris must have noticed.

"John, when you finish cleaning up why not come back to my office? I want to see you on some matters." Mr. Morris said to me as I was finishing up my Saturday afternoon tour at the counter.

I was suddenly jerked back into the present. What had I done wrong? Why did Mr. Morris want to see me? I finished my task at the counter, shed my white starched jacket and made my way to his office.

"Shut the door behind you," Mr. Morris instructed when I entered his office. Rarely did he shut his office door, and this only made my mounting anxiety greater. "Something's bothering you. What's going on? Do you want to talk it out?"

Mr. Morris was probably the only person who I could talk to. I hesitated. Did I really want to disclose to Mr. Morris what I was thinking? Could I trust him? What could he do?

Mr. Morris sat quietly and patiently at his desk, sensing that a lot was going through my mind. I slowly began to relate to him what I had done and Judge Allison's response.

"John, I've been meaning to talk to you about college for some time. Now is a good time to start." With that Mr. Morris told me about Northwestern University, in Evanston, Illinois, which was a short distance from Chicago.

I knew that Northwestern was his alma mater, so I was not surprised. Then, he explained that Northwestern was one of the original universities that the Navy had selected for the Regular Naval NROTC program and that the Navy was the only branch of the military where you could get a regular commission. To get a regular commission in the Army you had to go to West Point. Somehow, the Navy, way back in 1926, had been able to get through Congress an act that allowed it to offer scholarships to young men to attend a regular university. You were enrolled in the Navy NROTC program as a Midshipman, and went on the summer cruises just like the Midshipmen at Annapolis and got a regular appointment as an officer in the U.S. Navy, just like Annapolis.

"To get a Navy scholarship is highly competitive, thousands of young men apply each year and only several hundred are selected. You have to pass an academic exam first and then pass a rigid physical exam. But it does not require a political appointment. Everyone has a fair chance. I just think you might be able to win one of the scholarships," Mr. Morris said encouragingly, with a big smile across his face.

"Why not go for it? You have nothing to lose and who knows."

Midshipman. . .summer cruises. . .a regular appointment as an officer in the U.S. Navy. . .Chicago. . . . .city of broad shoulders. . .I felt better already. I imagined myself off to Northwestern on the next Greyhound. Not that I knew anything about Northwestern, but if Mr. Morris had gone there it had to be a good school.

Mr. Morris must have sensed that I was about to pack my bags. He seemed to have pretty good sensors when it came to me. Maybe he had those same good sensors for all of us whom he had pulled off Pine

Street, and put behind his soda fountain counter. I never knew what he said to Bob or Donald, who were my contemporaries behind the counter. But it didn't matter. Mr. Morris seemed to be around at the crucial times when I needed some guidance and counsel from someone other than my folks.

"Now, not quite so fast, John," he cautioned. "We need to do some planning. You first have to get information from Northwestern about their academic program. Although, when you win the Navy scholarship there are any number of universities you can go to. I hope you will seriously look at Northwestern. You and I could even visit the campus if you want to. I would be happy to take you there myself. But that will have to wait until you have gone through the process of winning a Navy scholarship. Go on down to the Navy recruiting office and pick up an application. I am sure they have some in their files."

I was off and running. But first I asked Mr. Morris to keep this between the two of us. Don't even mention it to my Dad. I didn't want to raise expectations, even with my folks, and then have something happen. Not pass the academic tests or the physical exam. Not get selected. Not get into Northwestern. Any number of things that might go wrong. We agreed that it was our project, the two of us, and that he would help guide me through the process.

MOVIN' ON

ON A COLD DAY IN EARLY FEBRUARY, I drove myself to Jefferson City, the State Capitol, to take the Navy's academic exam. Fortunately, there had been no recent ice storm that passes for winter in the Ozarks, making the highways slick and dangerous. It was a bright cold clear blue sky day. I was thankful for such a day. My spirits began to soar, overcoming the knot in my stomach. I endured several hours of grinding exams, testing whether I had what it took. I apparently did okay, for about a month later I received an official letter from the U.S. Navy announcing that I had passed the academic exam and must now report to the Navy Recruiting Center in St. Louis for my physical exam. This turned out to be a horse of a different color.

It was time to confess to my folks what I was up to. They were surprised, to say the least. They had always assumed that I would be a Miner come the next fall, close to home, affordable, a known commodity and all that. It had been a long time since anyone in our family had served in the military. The Civil War in fact. But the thought of having a son serving in the U.S. Navy as a regular officer seemed to appeal to Dad. He gave me a great big smile when he congratulated me for passing the first set of tests. Mother seemed somewhat more reserved in her enthusiasm. She had long hoped that I would become a writer, not a Navy officer. Dad took a day off from the garage and drove me to St. Louis for my physical exam.

This time it was not a clear blue sky day. It was cold and icy, grey and foreboding. We carefully made our way down the highway and into central St. Louis where the Navy Recruiting and Examination Offices were located. I checked in. Dad said he would return in about four hours. I was led away by a Navy medic to a large room full of other guys my age, going through the same process. It seemed that there were hundreds of them, all eager and willing to seize my scholarship. We were divided up into small groups to speed up the process of checking out our vitals.

I was weighed, measured, and then led off to be examined for hernia and other disorders of the lower region. I learned from others standing in the long line that this was known as the "gonad check." I had been examined for possible hernia, in Rolla, but Dr. Myers never told me it was a gonad check. I simply stood in front of him while he stuck his finger up one side of my privates, told me to turn my head to the other side and cough and then repeat the process on the other side of my privates. I didn't give this part of my Navy physical much thought. That was until the rumor suddenly began spreading down the line. It was a rumor that sent shudders up and down our spines.

"That Navy doctor checking our gonads is a WOMAN!"

"A woman!"

"A woman doctor?"

"Yeah."

"And, what's more, some poor slob had his thing go straight up when she probed him."

"You got to be kidding."

"Not on a bet. Straight up. No kidding."

"What do we do?"

"Better think of her as your mother when you get there, and keep your mind focused on other things."

"Your mother! How's that going to help?"

"Got any better ideas?"

As we slowly worked our way up the line, closing in on the dreaded ordeal of being examined by a woman doctor, the tension rose. Suddenly, I found myself facing the large white curtain drawn across the examination site with a Navy medic standing guard outside.

"Wilson, John Oliver, social security number xxx-xx-xxxx?"

"Yes, sir."

"Step inside. Drop your drawers. Proceed through the next curtain. Next!"

I parted the curtains and "dropped my drawers." Then, I parted the next set of curtains. Seated before me was a woman in a white medical jacket with a plastic badge reading Dr. Joyce C. Meadows. She looked to be in her mid-twenties, her brown hair pulled back in a tight bun, wearing wire-rimmed glasses. She spoke in a very official tone.

"Step forward son."

"Yes, Ma'am."

"Doctor will do."

"Yes, sir."

She probed. I turned and coughed, then turned to the other side. She probed again. I coughed.

"He's all there," she said to the Navy medic standing beside her holding a clipboard where my name must have been listed with the hundreds of others who were out to take my scholarship.

"Move on. Next." the medic ordered.

It happened so fast I didn't even have time to think of Dr.

Meadows as my mother, or think of anything else, for that matter. I was off and running. Or I should say standing in a long line again, waiting to see if my ticker was functioning, my eyes were reliable, and my reflexes were adequate.

Four hours later I was dressed, shivering on the corner, waiting for Dad to appear for the long drive over icy roads back to Rolla.

"How did it go?" Dad asked once we were on the road.

"Interesting," was all I responded.

The days began to turn into weeks. Several weeks, in fact. Then, the official letter from the U.S. Navy arrived.

"Dear Mr. John Oliver Wilson. . .We are happy to inform you that you have been selected as a Regular NROTC candidate. . ."

I sat stunned. Sitting at my desk in the security of my bedroom, I read the letter again. And then read it once more. I wanted to bite into it to see if it was real, much as old prospectors bit into gold. I held it up to the light of my window to make sure the type would not disappear. I carefully put it on my desk, face up, got up out of my chair and slowly paced around my bedroom.

I stood looking out the window at our side yard, where I had first played catch with Dad, and then with neighborhood kids. I saw the treehouse I had built in a big elm tree next to the garage. I thought about all the times I had mowed and raked our yard. I recalled the hot humid days that Dad and I had spent working together putting on a new roof, new siding, repairing window sills, and building a new front porch. I remembered all the other things we had done together to turn a run-down farmhouse into something for raising a family. I thought about Cocoa our bird dog, now buried in the backyard, his still vacant doghouse sitting behind the garage where he and I had bonded so many years ago. I thought of my canoe sitting on its ropes hanging from the rafters in the garage, waiting to be lowered to the top of the old Plymouth coupe Shorty Johnson and the other mechanics at the garage had rebuilt and given to me on my sixteenth birthday. There would be no more slow meandering floats down the Gasconade in the "great green monster."

I recalled all the people who had nurtured and guided my growing up in Rolla: the Whites, and the Smiths, and George Christopher who had taught me to box, and Millard Underwood, best friend all the way from second grade through high school, Shorty Johnson and the other mechanics at the garage, Johnnie Morris and Scott's Drugstore.

I was heading to the great big city of Chicago, a stormy, husky, brawling city of broad shoulders, to Northwestern and the challenge of putting my mind up against others, to the Navy NROTC unit and life as a Midshipman, to summer cruises and a commission as a regular officer with my own bright sword to wear down my side in my own dress white uniform. It was time to move on.

TALL TALES AND NO LIES

john oliver wilson

Tall Tales and No Lies

TALL TALES AND NO LIES

john oliver wilson

Please send me:
TALL TALES AND NO LIES
ISBN 978-1-877809-35-4

Number of books _____ @ $14.00 each   = _____

Sales Tax (add 7.75% for books shipped to CA) = _____

Shipping/Handling (add $2.50 per book)   = _____

Add $1 for each add'l book to same address   = _____

Total Enclosed   = _____

Check or money order payable to John O. Wilson

Send books to (please print)

Name _____

Address _____

City _____

State, Zip _____

Send your payment with this order form to:

John O. Wilson, P.O. Box 507, St. Helena, CA 94574

Books shipped immediately upon receipt of order.

COMMENTS:_____

_____

_____

_____